THIS WON'T
BE PRETTY

Emily —
   Keep being the
amazing woman
   you are!

                  C.

Published by Grammar Factory Publishing, an imprint of MacMillan Company Limited.

Grammar Factory Publishing
MacMillan Company Limited
25 Telegram Mews, 39th Floor, Suite 3906
Toronto, Ontario, Canada
M5V 3Z1

www.grammarfactory.com

D'Alessio, Cassandra, 1985–
    This Won't be Pretty: First Year Lessons for the Female Entreprenur/Cassandra D'Alessio

ISBN 978-1-989737-12-5
eBook: 978-1-989737-13-2

1. BUS025000 Business & Economics / Entrepreneurship. 2. BUS060000 Business & Economics / Small Business. 3. SEL027000 SELF-HELP / Personal Growth / Success.

Production Credits
Printed in Canada
Cover design by Designerbility
Interior layout design by Dania Zafar
Book production and editorial services by Grammar Factory Publishing

Disclaimer
The material in this publication is of the nature of general comment only and does not represent professional advice. It is not intended to provide specific guidance for particular circumstances, and it should not be relied on as the basis for any decision to take action or not take action on any matter which it covers. Readers should obtain professional advice where appropriate, before making any such decision. To the maximum extent permitted by law, the author and publisher disclaim all responsibility and liability to any person, arising directly or indirectly from any person taking or not taking action based on the information in this publication.

THIS WON'T BE PRETTY

FIRST-YEAR LESSONS FOR THE FEMALE ENTREPRENEUR

CASSANDRA D'ALESSIO

For Gammy

"Find out who you are and do it on purpose."

Dolly Parton

Contents

Let's Turn the Next Page

Once upon a time, before I had a business of my own and was the successful, confident woman I am today, I was at a low point in my life. And I mean *low*: I had just gotten divorced from my husband of five years, I had been evicted from my apartment due to new construction being built on the land, and my contract position as a lecturer at a university had ended and was not going to be renewed.

I was thirty years old, and if I didn't do anything about it fast, I was going to end up homeless, jobless, and still healing from the dissolution of my marriage. I wasn't prepared to return home as a "failed" thirty-year-old to my family, who were 475 miles away. This meant that I would have to hustle, and that I would have to trust the universe, believing that everything would work out.

I really, *really* didn't want to do that.

All I wanted was to have stability. I wanted to know for certain what was going to happen. I only wanted to have to worry about everyday things, like "Am I due for an oil change?" Normal stuff. Not the stuff I was dealing with, like "Where am I going to find another place to live?" and "How am I going to pay for it if I don't have a job?" But I had no choice. I had no guarantee for what was to come. So, I told myself I would get through this time *because* I didn't have a choice. I built grit. I gained the courage and resolve needed to keep moving forward instead of becoming swallowed up by events (mostly) out of my control. During this painful transition, I learned to adapt to my surroundings. I grew a thicker skin, so that whenever a big issue came up (like when I rear-ended a police car at a red light), it wasn't something I fell to pieces over. It simply happened. I would sigh heavily, laugh slightly (because, of course, I had just rear-ended a police car at a red light), and then I would take responsibility without becoming overwhelmed with worry.

I also learned to trust. Not just myself, and the people around me, but the universe, too. I remember lying on my mat in a hot yoga class when the instructor told us to feel the ground beneath us – and explained how, no matter what was in flux or uncertain in our lives right now, the ground was there, and always would be. That was the first moment I remember feeling truly grounded (no pun intended). The earth was there. There was something solid beneath me, even if I didn't feel solid at all. That's approximately the moment I learned to trust again. When all else might fail, I could at least trust that the ground would still support me.

All these lessons, all these changes that had made me into a stronger person during this difficult time – I didn't know it then, but they would end up shaping me into the kind of person who would want to become an entrepreneur.

WHERE I BEGAN

In the year and months that followed my divorce, the loss of my dream job, and my eviction from my apartment, I became a different person. And although I didn't realize it at the time, this was the type of person who was meant to be an entrepreneur.

If I were to go back to that past version of myself (before those events) and tell her that she would be running her own business now – and a successful one at that – she wouldn't believe me. Start my own business? She would be exhausted just saying the phrase. Run my business as the sole leader? Take on the financial risk? Hustle day in and day out to make sure money keeps coming in even when there's a strong possibility it won't and I might end up failing? "No thanks," she would say. "Being unstable is awful. Why would I consciously choose that?"

But she didn't know who she was yet. She didn't know what she was capable of, after having experienced that difficult period in her life. That person who had survived the end of that year, who had put her faith in the universe when she could, she had gone through a lot, and would end up stronger and more independent than ever.

Not that it was a perfect transition. Not at all; it was messy. I was alone – a lot. I cried – a lot. I drank wine and ate Cool Ranch Doritos every night for months and slept every moment that I could. But at some point, I put all my energy into researching jobs across the country because nothing was tying me to Charlotte, North Carolina, where I was living. That change that I had to trust to come did, eventually, come. By spring of the next year, I was working as the Director of Marketing at an organization that empowered women, where I worked alongside amazing role models. Two months after that, I bought a condo. Stability had finally found me. It was the safety net I had been waiting for.

But, after having gone through so much, I wanted more. Stability was no longer the only thing I wanted. I wanted to be happy, and I wanted to live my life my way.

It's funny, isn't it, when you search for the thing you believe will bring you happiness, and then it shockingly doesn't satisfy you once you have it? I had stability, but I wasn't happy. Eventually, I found that my new work environment felt eerily similar to the toxic marriage I had just left. At first, I felt like I had hit the jackpot. I was complimented ferociously by women in the leadership above me. My ego was stroked and I felt I was a trusted part of the team. Then, I would hear comments about other employees from these same women who were complimenting me to my face. The comments were cruel and petty. I began to feel very insecure and distrustful of the leadership above me. I began to look at their overzealous compliments as manipulation tools, and I was careful about every decision I made – professional or otherwise – so it couldn't be used against me in the future. It felt like a bad relationship, like the one I had just left, all over again.

So, what happens when you find yourself in another bad relationship? Well, you either blame yourself and that you're "just being overly sensitive," or you get angry and say, "Screw. This." And if I was able to do that with my ex-husband, whom I had lived with for seven years, I could certainly do it with someone I only saw Monday through Friday. Which is exactly what I did. The old me would have never done this. She would have continued to work and adapt to whatever was needed of her to keep the job she had – and had so desperately wished for. But the new me was not having it. I was tired, annoyed, and, most of all, angry. So, one September morning, as I was pulling into the parking lot at work, I made a decision: I would give my official notice after Thanksgiving, then start the New Year with a new chapter, even if I didn't know what was going to be on that page.

At first, I did the "normal" exit planning someone does when they're ready to leave their job. I began searching for openings in my industry at other organizations. I had coffees and lunches with people I knew in those organizations. I scanned LinkedIn, looking for connections that might be my entry point. I learned about the work culture of different organizations and read GlassDoor reviews. Then, one afternoon, while I was calling in to do yet another phone interview during my lunch break in my car, something occurred to me. What if I found myself in this same position in a year? Or two years? Or ten? Statistically, I was unlikely to stay at this next job for the rest of my life. According to the Bureau of Labor, the average person changes jobs twelve times during their life.[1] So, why was I working so hard to do this very "normal" thing of finding another desk job when I wasn't even convinced it would bring me happiness? That's when I realized there was another option. I didn't have to work for anyone else. I could work for me.

After everything I had gone through, I knew what I wanted, and I was ready for the transition. I was ready for something new. I had been ready for this, perhaps, my entire life.

BECOMING AN ENTREPRENEUR

If you're reading this book, chances are you connect with this story. Maybe you're frustrated at your current job, but the thought of researching a new job is not exciting. Maybe you've watched other friends or family members take the entrepreneurial leap and you've been curious about it for yourself. Maybe you've even gone as far as to create a company name and purchase the web address – just in case. And perhaps, no matter what stage you're in, just like me when I was first starting, you don't know what you're getting into or where to even begin.

Becoming an entrepreneur might not be something you were born to do – but now, life has shaped you to become one. So, you feel like it's time to take the leap, just like I did that September morning

---

[1] "Number of Jobs, Labor Market Experience, and Earnings Growth: Results from a National Longitudinal Survey." *www.bls.gov/nls*, 22 Aug. 2019, www.bls.gov/news.release/pdf/nlsoy.pdf.

in my car. But maybe, just like I did, you still have some fears. Okay, maybe you have lots of fears. Does any of this sound familiar?

How will I pay for health insurance?
How will I save for retirement?
How will I find clients?
How will I know what to charge?
What will happen if a client doesn't pay me?
What kind of taxes will I need to pay as a business owner?
What will happen if I lose a client?
What if I fail?

That's why I've written this book. I've had to deal with these worries, and I've had to face all kinds of challenges – many of them unexpected. But if there's anything I've learned, it's that I could get through it. And you can, too.

THIS WON'T BE PRETTY

In this book, you'll learn about all the different challenges that can come up during your first year of running a business – and how to face them. You'll also learn how to get ready for that big step of starting out, and how to continue to grow your business once you've gone through the transition of becoming an entrepreneur. By joining me on the journey of my first year as an entrepreneur and beyond, you can learn from my mistakes and do a little better on your own entrepreneurial journey.

My journey and lessons learned will be covered in the following chapters:

Chapter 1: Get Your House in Order: In this chapter, we'll review the first steps you'll need to take when starting your business, like finding a productive workspace.

Chapter 2: Get Your Business Ready: In this chapter, we'll discuss branding and how to develop the idea of your business.

Chapter 3: Get Yourself in Order: In this chapter, we'll look at creating office hours, setting a schedule, and other effective strategies you can use to avoid feeling overwhelmed or burned out.

Chapter 4: Get Your Business Out There: In this chapter, we'll discuss marketing to your ideal client.

Chapter 5: Get Yourself Out There: In this chapter, we'll review different strategies for building your network.

Chapter 6: Get to Know Other People: In this chapter, we'll talk about the types of people you'll meet while you are networking and how to incorporate them (or not) into your business.

Chapter 7: Set Your Boundaries: In this chapter, we'll talk about the importance of saying "no."

Chapter 8: Face the Setbacks: In this chapter, we'll discuss the inevitable failures that come with owning a business and how you can move forward successfully.

Going through these chapters, you'll learn everything you need to become the entrepreneur you want to be. My hope is that when you get to the end of this book, you'll feel confident that you can accomplish the same goals for your business as I did for my own.

However, keep this in mind: My goals did *not* include working 150 hours a week so I could build a multi-million-dollar empire and end up with my name on the side of my own private jet. That would be sweet, but I'm not willing to sacrifice my time and health (more on that later) to make that happen.

I had clear goals going into owning my own business. If this is the type of business owner you aim to be, then we're going to get along very well:

1. Be my own boss
2. Have a flexible schedule
3. Make enough money to maintain my current lifestyle (including paying for a mortgage and keeping my dog fed)
4. Continue to invest in my retirement
5. Have the freedom to try different things in my career

I know that you can make it happen. From my experience as an entrepreneur, I have accomplished much more than I could have ever anticipated. At the time of writing this book, almost three years into owning my business, I have closed over $130,000 in sales without any previous sales training. I have doubled my net salary every year, making far more than I did during my days as a university lecturer. I've been a guest speaker at university panels, in networking groups, and on several podcasts. And I, a self-described introvert, have grown my circle of trusted friends dozens of times over.

I'm not going to promise that it will be easy. And it's certainly not going to be pretty – growth never is. In fact, starting a business is a little like jumping into adulthood, because you think you should know how to do it, but you really don't, and the universe is going to kick you in the butt a bit to see if you truly belong in this place.

I won't promise that this book will make your first year painless – that's not the point. If you're not experiencing some pain, then you're not learning anything. Being an entrepreneur isn't all napping in the afternoon and wearing yoga pants every day. It's about hard work and some (okay, maybe a lot of) sleepless nights and self-doubt. It's also about learning your limits and asking for help when you need it. It's about taking charge of your finances and becoming organized about your spending.

And it's also about learning who you are. It's about discovering your unrealized talents. It's about answering only to yourself at the end of the day. It's about uncovering your strength, which, I promise, you have more of than you could ever imagine. It's about starting something that most people (especially women) are afraid to try. It's about earning success that *no one else* can take credit for.

Ready? Let's turn the next page.

1

Get Your House in Order

When I started my business, back in 2017, I was entering a huge transitional period in my life. I was leaving a stable job for insecurity. I was taking a risk that I'd never thought I would be capable of taking. I was starting my journey as an entrepreneur with lots of trust in the world and a lot of drive – but I didn't know what to expect. My new business was like a house I was building from the ground up, but without any plans to guide me. I could see only the foundation, and I didn't know what the building would look like in a year's time. I didn't even have the tools I needed to build the whole thing. To be honest, I didn't even know what those tools were or where I was going to find them.

If I'd had those tools, I would have done a few things differently. First, I would have carved out a *dedicated* workspace in my home much sooner. Second, I would have read some really boring books on taxes and what to expect when the government comes calling so I wouldn't have to feel rattled to my core come April. And third, I would have set up one central meeting place so I wouldn't have to crisscross the city to meet with new people.

These are just a few reasons why it's so important to get your house in order, even before you've begun your entrepreneurial journey. Some of the ways you'll want to prepare are by:

1. Finding an adequate (and productive) workspace
2. Knowing your budget
3. Creating a schedule that works for you

FINDING AN ADEQUATE (AND PRODUCTIVE) WORKSPACE

As an introvert, I value the quiet and comfort of my house. So, naturally, working from home made sense for me when I started my business. But there was still a lot I had to learn about working in that environment. One mistake I made was not having a dedicated workspace as my office. When I started out, my office wasn't just an office, but also a yoga/meditation/guest room. After about eight months, I found myself not wanting to do yoga in the same place I was doing work. And I couldn't really concentrate on work when I was thinking about doing yoga. To fix this problem, I scheduled classes with my local yoga studio so I would have to leave my house completely, or I practiced yoga in a different room of the house.

I also read how to "feng shui" your office and made important adjustments to my space. First, I moved the desk away from the wall, so it was facing the middle of the room. *Never face a wall*, I'd read, *it dampens your energy.* Uh, sure. But after moving my desk there, my productivity skyrocketed. If I sat down at my desk with the sole purpose of reading only one email, an hour or so would suddenly go by without my knowing it because I had been pulled into some project. Then, I ensured I had adequate table and floor lamps in order to bring *a warm, grounding glow* to the room. No overhead lighting. Finally, I made sure my laptop, desk, and chair were ergonomically supportive of my hips and neck so that I wouldn't be hunched over my keyboard or – worse – lying against an ice pack every night because of poor posture.

I also took everything that wasn't work-related out of my office – except for my dog's toys, because even I can't stop him from leaving those everywhere. That way, I wouldn't have anything unrelated to work distracting me.

Finally, after several months of trial and error (and some neck aches), I had a dedicated (and productive) workspace. I felt confident when I walked into that room in the morning. And I felt like I had completed a real day of work when I left in the evening. Finding the right workspace and making it work for you can make a huge difference to both the success of your business and how happy you are at the office. Otherwise, you can end up feeling unfocused or overwhelmed.

In 2020, when nearly every corporate employee moved to a work-from-home environment during the COVID-19 pandemic, the popular phrase "living at work" arose to describe what people were doing instead of "working from home." This problem of "living at work" is very common for entrepreneurs in their first year of business. So, you need to do your best to keep your work life and real life separate – fortunately, creating the right workspace is a great strategy for achieving this balance.

DIFFERENT WORKSPACE OPTIONS

Different workspaces work for different people. Just because working from home worked for me – that doesn't mean that it will suit your personality and work style. Luckily, there are lots of options out there, including:

1. Coworking spaces
2. Coffee Shops
3. Bookstores, Libraries, and More
4. Working from Home

Coworking Spaces

If you've worked in an office space before and enjoyed it, then you're probably one of those people who needs interaction with others. Thankfully, coworking spaces give you exactly that. They are relatively cheap for starting entrepreneurs, and there are various options available depending on what you're looking for. In my second year, I rented an office in a coworking space for entrepreneurs. Although it was in a coworking space filled with other people, my office had its own door, so I had the privacy I needed to be productive. The offices in that building, which was about a mile outside the center of Charlotte, NC, ran between $350 to $550 a month. This runs on the low-end of what a coworking space usually costs, mainly because my building did not offer other perks like some of the more well-known coworking spaces. For a dedicated desk (let alone an office with a door), a working space in a major city is going to cost at least $200 and could cost upwards of $1,100 a month.

Other coworking spaces have a variety of options with varying degrees of privacy. Renting a desk or "floating desk" could cost anywhere between $100-$300 per month, while a private office in that same building could run upwards of $700+ per month. However, you get what you pay for. And, depending on how much you plan to use the amenities, it may be worth the extra cash. My office rent included the space I was using, Wi-Fi, the use of the kitchen, and other basic amenities. Other, branded coworking spaces, with spaces all over the city or country, might offer any of the following:

1. Conference rooms
2. A podcast studio
3. Large event spaces
4. An on-site gym and showers
5. Free coffee
6. An on-site food truck or restaurant
7. Creative spaces with white boards
8. Comfortable couches, chairs, and other inspiring areas

Depending on your type of business and how many people you expect to have in your space, whether clients, a hired team, etc., a coworking space could definitely be an option for you.

Coffee Shops

Some people enjoy the vibe of coffee shops. You would be hard pressed to find a coffee spot without half a dozen people on laptops, earbuds in, typing furiously. So, if that's your thing, this is a great option for you. Like with working from a coworking space, this option requires that you factor their costs into what you can afford every month. Even a coffee house isn't really free. Sure, you *could* sit there without buying anything, using up their free Wi-Fi, but that's bad karma. I recommend you support the business that's supporting yours. The $2.75 for a cup of coffee will not break you.

Bookstores, Libraries and More

Of course, if you're not a fan of coffee or tea, there are options similar to a coffee shop that provide you with a productive workspace. Many bookstores – with or without a coffee shop – are a great option. Don't overlook your local library either. It's a free, quiet space for you to be productive. Depending on your tolerance for distractions, some casual restaurants and bars are open earlier in the day and could also provide a space away from your home to be productive.

The most important thing to remember is that you need to find an environment that will work for you. Some entrepreneurs cannot work in complete quiet. Others crave it. Some need to feel as though they are still in an "office" setting with others working around them. Others can create a productive workspace in the middle of a park.

Working from Home

If you're like me and you're too easily distracted when people are around, working from home is the most productive workspace option. It's not for everyone, especially if you A) don't have a dedicated workspace or B) can't stop yourself from binge-watching TV shows on Netflix or watching a movie in the middle of the day. But if you thrive in a quiet environment, are a natural homebody and – let's be honest here – an introvert, then working from home will feel like the best option. However, once you are working from home, you'll soon realize that your home life and work life, which were once separated by miles, are now intertwined. To maintain a productive workspace, I recommend the following:

- ✓ Set office hours for yourself, including a scheduled lunch break.
- ✓ Have the ability to close a door or put away your laptop at the end of the day. (Your office should never be 100 per cent accessible.)
- ✓ Ensure you have the technology needed to be productive: a printer, strong Wi-Fi, and a Bluetooth speaker or headset.

KNOW YOUR NUMBERS

I was never good at math. I excelled in English, sure. But numbers? No, thank you. This was (kind of) okay for most of my adult life since I always had a steady job and income coming in, so I didn't have to worry much then about budgeting. I have never been an extravagant spender, so that probably saved me. When I decided to start my business, I reviewed my monthly expenses (my mortgage, utilities, groceries, dog meds, and so on) to determine how much savings I had to support me if no other money was coming in. I had three months.

Those three months came and went, and I had clients paying me. They weren't paying a lot, but I still had some money coming in. In fact, I was doing mostly okay until I hit that first summer about six months after I started my business. Business typically slows during the summer, especially in North Carolina. Come August, my bank account was keeping me up at night. I started to cut back on my grocery budget. I didn't buy my favorite shampoo or face wash anymore. I switched to a cheaper, albeit less fun, option (bottled water) when I visited coffee shops. Considering how well I'd managed my money before becoming an entrepreneur, I was surprised at the cuts I had to make.

To keep yourself from ending up in this same situation, this is what I suggest you do:

When you're first looking at your current expenses before starting a business, add twenty per cent. Even though I now have a set salary that I earn from my business, I still add a cushion of twenty per cent. Once you start earning, you should move this additional twenty per cent into a savings account for house or car emergencies. Or you can move it into a high-yield savings account for an IRA investment later. In my case, I decided to always have a "Three Month Backup." I created a savings account that included three months' worth of expenses that I could live on if my business suddenly disappeared. To this day, I always ensure I have that safety net.

Knowing what your personal spending habits are is incredibly important for understanding how you are going to build your business. It's also important to know what your risk tolerance is for going frugal, since the higher this tolerance is, the (slightly) less painful this transition will be. Because, at the end of the day, you need to survive. To do this, you'll need to know how much you need to make per month to break even.

I know what you're thinking. I want to make money, not just break even. Trust me: You are going to be really lucky if you break even during your first year. And when you start out, you're going to have to get by month to month (if not week to week... and, sometimes, day to day). Once you're able to shift your mindset toward the idea of not receiving a paycheck every two weeks (it's a tough one, no matter how resilient you are), you need to figure out how much money you *need*, and also how much money it would be nice to have to maintain your lifestyle. Chances are, that lifestyle is going to shift dramatically, if only for a moment. That's what happened to me, even though I've always been frugal with money. I enjoy cooking my own meals, I rarely go shopping, and I steal Netflix from my sister and brother-in-law – yet, I was still forced to make some changes to my lifestyle when I started my business.

There's an exercise at the end of this chapter to help you establish your budget. However, here are some big-picture strategies for budgeting that you should begin to consider now:

How much money do you spend every month on what you need to survive?

1. Housing
2. Utilities
3. Car/Transportation
4. Food

What expenses do you need to plan for as an entrepreneur?

1. Health Insurance (unless you are a dependent on someone else's insurance, you will need to purchase this yourself – go to www.HealthCare.gov for more details)
2. Taxes
3. Technology (reliable computer, printer, software?)
4. Networking costs to attend events (either virtual or in person)
5. Coffee (so much coffee)
6. Coworking space or other rental space

Finally, what are the other expenses you pay for right now where you can trim the fat?

1. Memberships (gym, yoga, wine club, and so on)
2. Subscription services
3. Favorite shops
4. Pedicures/Manicures
5. Vacations
6. Other expensive hobbies

There will be a more in-depth exercise at the end of this chapter, but for now, jot down an idea of how much each of these areas currently cost. A general idea of how much money you are currently spending is a good place to start. The details can come later.

OFFICE HOURS AND MORE

When I first started working from home and without a boss, it was a big mind shift. Suddenly, it felt like I had the time to do whatever I wanted, whenever I wanted. Head to the outlet mall for a new blazer? Definitely. Yoga class in the middle of the day? Heck yeah. Get a haircut on a Tuesday morning? Sure! But those are working hours, and just because I had the flexibility to do the things I wanted to do (or needed to do) during the weekday, that didn't mean that the rest of the world had stopped adhering to the conventional 8am-5pm, Monday-Friday mindset. I learned that, although it was tempting to "splurge" my time, it was better to save my time, like an entrepreneurial camel.

I learned this lesson the hard way when I took a vacation only three months into owning my business. It was way too soon. But I didn't know that, because it was my first official vacation as a self-employed person, and I thought I was completely prepared. I brought my client folders. I brought my laptop. I brought my laptop charger. I told my clients I would be available by phone for emergencies, and that I would get to my emails as I was able. I switched on my "out of office" and thought it would be smooth sailing.

This did not go well. The mistake of bad planning turned out to actually be four mistakes rolled in one:

First, since I was still figuring out boundaries with my clients, I didn't realize that they might not share the fact that I was "out of the office" with others on their team. So, when I got a call way too early one morning from a client's office number, I panicked – thinking it was an emergency. It wasn't. My client's colleague didn't know I was on vacation, because no one had told her I was.

Second, I didn't account for potential business partners calling me in the afternoon – on a Monday – when I would normally be holding business hours. I wasn't ready for that, because I wasn't in "business mode." I didn't have my calendar or computer in front of me. There may have been the sound of a jazz band playing in the background when I answered (sorry about that, William). But I had to answer, even though I wasn't in the best environment to do so. I couldn't allow that phone call to go to voicemail. I had to answer it because, if I didn't, who else would?

Third, my vacation had a negative effect on my business schedule. Usually, the beginning of the month is when I sit and take stock of where my finances are so I can create a game plan for the month. Going "back to the office" (home, in other words) on the seventh day of the month when my vacation was over meant I was seven days behind the curve. That's seven days of planning I hadn't done. That's seven days' worth of meetings I hadn't had. Hell, it was almost mid-month, and I was just starting to get my feet under me again.

Fourth, I didn't set aside legitimate "work time" while I was gone. I brought all my business materials with me, but I wasn't strict enough with myself (or my travel buddies) about the work I needed to complete. My clients were still working – despite my being on vacation – and things still needed to get done. By the time I came back home, I was completely frustrated with myself. Despite my good intention of planning to work while I was gone, I had been too disorganized and ill-prepared to actually make that happen.

Learn from my mistake. Whatever you do, please don't plan a vacation within the first ninety days of starting your business. Your sanity (and bank account) will not forgive you if you do. I know it's tempting to look at your calendar and believe you rule every hour of your day, but guess what? You don't. At least, not this early on. But the good news is that you can take some control of those hours and set some ground rules for yourself and your clients. The easiest way to do this is to get a reliable planner and begin creating a schedule that works for both you and your new business.

Get. A. Planner.

When I started building my business, I had to learn quickly how to maintain a new kind of balance. I wasn't used to hours of empty space that would be filled by only me. What I *was* used to were corporate, structured jobs. In a corporate job, our days are laid out for us in a system that we understand and accept. We need to be at work at a specific time, work for four hours, have a lunch break, then work another four hours until we wrap up and head home.

There are clear boundaries between our personal and work lives. Hell, there are even different clothes and personalities we put on for those two halves of our lives. When I became an entrepreneur, everything changed because I was no longer part of a system that helped me maintain balance.

As a result, I had to start over and come up with a new schedule. Otherwise, that vacation fiasco was just going to happen again. And building a business – on my own – made me feel like an octopus balancing multiple ceramic plates. Some plates were spinning. Some felt firmly in my grasp. But I felt off-balance, and even more so when unexpected things happened. Which happens a lot when you're running your own business. So, even though I felt prepared for and secure about my decision to begin a business, what I was *not* prepared for was how hectic and overwhelming my days would begin to feel almost immediately.

I had to come up with a solution. Very quickly, I figured out what worked for me: using a planner to schedule everything.

What began as me putting only meetings on my calendar and in my planner in year one had turned by year two into me breaking down almost every hour of my day and scheduling it in – including time I was taking for myself to do yoga, walk my dog, and eat lunch/watch one Netflix episode (just *one*). I scheduled it all. Everything. This not only gave physical structure to my days, but gave me mental and emotional structure as well, which was very calming. Even though I couldn't completely predict what my days or weeks would look like, I at least had a place to start. I could mentally and emotionally prepare myself for my days once they were no longer long stretches of "empty space" on my calendar.

Strategies for Organizing Your Planner

Depending on your organization style, different strategies will work for you when you're organizing your planner. I have an all-or-nothing mindset. Everything that goes into my digital calendar – calls, meetings, check-ins, and so on – is also hand-written into my hardcover planner. Other people might keep their brainstorming thoughts and reminders in their planner, with meetings and calls scheduled in their digital calendar. There is, of course, no one right way to approach organizing your new life, but it is important to try a few different methods in case you don't innately know.

If you're unsure, here are some options for how you can use your planner:

- ✓ Create a list for that day's or week's tasks
- ✓ Keep a list of business goals and ideas as they come to you
- ✓ Jot down meeting notes and brainstorming ideas
- ✓ Create sketches of organizational charts, new product or service ideas, and so on
- ✓ Keep a comprehensive list of meetings and your reflections

I color code all my tasks, too, because Organization Rules. But you don't need to go that far. You also don't have to get a day planner, a white board, and fifteen different colored pens if you don't want to, but you should make sure that you're doing what you can to fill the schedule on your calendar as much as possible.

Part of your time should be focused on building the business: networking, researching prospects, and webinars/training. Another part of your time should be dedicated to working inside the business: completing client projects, reviewing your finances, and managing your marketing. Finally, you also need to schedule time to take care of yourself – this includes having dinner with friends, enjoying a hobby, and just getting out of the office for a while.

I know self-care falls off our plates more quickly than anything else, but practice makes perfect. Some weeks it will be easier than others. After my second debilitating migraine in eight months (more on that later), I knew it was essential for my business to take care of myself. I would not survive if I didn't schedule time to do that.

When you first begin your business, you will likely feel overwhelmed in one of two ways. Either you have *so* much free time you don't know how to fill it, or you feel that there is so much to do that you are paralyzed on where to begin. Setting office hours, using a planner, and making sure that you include self-care as part of your busy schedule will help you move toward your new normal in a productive way.

End-of-Chapter Check-in

EXERCISE 1: FINDING AN ADEQUATE (AND PRODUCTIVE) WORKSPACE

1. In what environment are you most productive? One that has:
   a. Lots of activity and people
   b. Silence/minimal interruption
   c. Structure
   d. A mix of the above

If you answer A, C, or D, you should be looking for coworking spaces, coffee shops, restaurants and other places where people are. You might also want to consider reaching out to a fellow entrepreneur (whom you like and trust) to see if they are open to working together in the same space.

If you answer B, C or D, your cheapest and easiest option would be working from home, however, if you do not live alone, a library or bookstore might be a good alternative. Remember, if you decide to work from home, make sure your space is conducive to work. Keep any distractions (food, Netflix, wine) out of sight if you think you might be tempted. Or use those as a reward after completing a major item on your to-do list.

2. Create a list of must-haves for you to be successful. Do you have the following?
   a. Reliable laptop
   b. Printer
   c. Reliable Wi-Fi
   d. Bluetooth speaker or headset
   e. Second monitor (if that helps your productivity)

EXERCISE 2: KNOWING YOUR BUDGET

1. How much money do you need to make per month to break even? Answer the questions below to find out. Remember, when you're answering these questions, to exaggerate your answers to a. and b. This will make the process feel less of a shock to your system when you are practicing it.
   a. How much are your monthly bills [essentials]? (This includes rent, mortgage, utilities, groceries/take out, and so on.)
   b. How much are your monthly bills [non-essentials]? (This includes restaurants, fun, hobbies, and so on.)
   c. How many hours a week do you actually want to be working? (This does not include networking or one-to-one meetings for building your brand reputation.)
   d. How much do you need to bill per hour to cover your monthly costs?

Next, add up the total amount of expenses you expect to have every month. If you can, cut out any non-essential items. What is the number of your total expenses per month?

Then, divide that number by how many hours you plan to work each month. (These are the hours that you are able to bill; in other words, you are completing client-specific projects versus attending a networking event which you cannot charge to a client.) This is your hourly rate.

Your next step is to research where this lands in your city and in your industry. Do a general internet search but also talk with others in your industry if you are comfortable, and possibly reach out to a business coach. Get some outside perspective on what you should be charging. You may have an advanced degree or special certification that others in your field don't have. How does that translate to more value for your clients?

Remember: It's important to budget for a lot of spending and saving. I understand that, at first, this will feel weird. It's your business and your money. Why shouldn't you do whatever you want with it? Here's why: If you don't feed the business with the money you are bringing in, and instead use it as a very large checking account, you are not a business owner. Think of your business as a child or other dependent. The less you keep for yourself, the more you can give to it. Your business needs money to thrive. For it to thrive, you need to go without.

EXERCISE 3: CREATING A SCHEDULE THAT WORKS FOR YOU

1. What type of calendar or planner is best for you?
   a. Digital
   b. Hardbound
   c. Large form (on a wall, a whiteboard, a desk, or similar)
   d. All of the above

You can choose D or a combination of A to C but you have to choose something. There are no exceptions to this. Your clients will expect you to be organized, even if they themselves are not. You might not need to be as color-conscious as I am or need to block out time for work versus play, but you should start somewhere. Even if it's just: "These are my office hours."

2

Get Your Business Ready

I n early 2017, before I had considered the idea of running my own business, I was talking to a friend, complaining about the petty office politics and toxic culture at the office where I was working. After I'd finished complaining, he said to me:

"You could just start your own business. You're smart. It would be easy."

"But what about health care?" I asked.

"There's plenty of options for entrepreneurs," he replied. He was one. It was the kind of thing he would know.

"Okay, well, I don't even know what I would need to do first."

"You just need to go Uptown and file the name of your business. Make sure no one else has it."

"And then what?"

"Just start a website."

"And then what?"

"Find clients."

"What if I lose a client?"

"Then you find another one."

His answers were annoyingly simplistic, but I'd had just enough wine to believe that his idea seemed possible. It was only a series of steps, and, what the hell – if I failed or hated it, it would still be better (and healthier) than the situation I was in at work.

Turns out, he was right. Not only was it possible for me to start my own business (obviously, since you're reading this book), but it was also a simple process, just a series of steps I had to take to get started. And this is a good way to think about the day-to-day tasks of owning a business. On any given day, there will always be a lot of things to do, but once you break it down into a series of steps, and you complete the "worst" task first thing in the morning, every day won't feel so overwhelming.

The best piece of advice here is to just "eat the frog." I first heard this in a networking group years after I began my business, but it's a fairly common phrase among entrepreneurs. Mark Twain allegedly once said, "Eat a live frog first thing in the morning." Then, he reasoned, "nothing worse can happen to you for the rest of the day." Brian Tracy adopted this mindset in his book *Eat That Frog!* Even if you don't consider yourself a procrastinator (and especially if you do), it's important to take steps to focus your to-do list. Because the to-do list of an entrepreneur is ever growing and there is seemingly never enough time to get everything done. Guess what? There will never be more time. As Tracy states, "Successful people don't try to do everything." Instead, it's about creating a very narrow focus for your day and tackling the hurdles that are most critical to your business development, starting with your least favorite task.[1]

In this chapter, you'll learn the basics of setting up your business, a preliminary step you need to take before you start engaging with clients and networking. Getting your business ready will include understanding:

1. How to define your business
2. Bookkeeping 101
3. How to ask for additional help

---

[1] Tracy, Brian. *Eat That Frog!* BBC, 2008.

HOW TO DEFINE YOUR BUSINESS

After the conversation I'd had with my friend about starting a business, I decided this was what I wanted to do. I wanted to start a business. But what kind of business? First, I had to think about the different services I could offer, how much I could charge, and how many hours I would be working a week. As a marketing director and former writing teacher, I had a lot of skills to offer. I also had many options in terms of what business services I could provide, from anything as generic as marketing consulting to as specific as blog writing and SEO support for IT services based in the Charlotte, North Carolina, area. In the end, I decided to offer content marketing services (blogs, social media, and brand messaging) for small businesses. Once I'd decided on what services I was providing, I was ready to think about my business name and what I'd want my business website and logo to look like.

As an emerging entrepreneur, it's important for you to understand what your business will "look" like to others. This includes knowing what services you're offering (and at what cost), how to develop your business strategy, who your ideal client is, and what to name your business.

This may be a good time to consider a marketing strategist or branding consultant. They can help you match what is in your head to what it will look like on paper, to your audience. I do this often when it comes to brand messaging for clients. A client who is a superstar in their industry might get hung up on specific words and phrases that they insist speak to their brand. But the truth is, unless you are doing business with others who are also professionals in your field, they are unlikely going to know (or understand) the jargon that relates to your business. Your clients want to know something more specific: How is your business going to help them? They want to *feel good* about your brand. Not confused. Confusion doesn't lead to sales.

Your Services

There's the familiar adage that you can't be all things to all people. At least not well. This will never be truer than when you're an entrepreneur because you'll have so many options available to you. I know I did. My experience was in marketing, and I wanted to start a marketing company. There were at least a dozen services I could provide that I had direct experience with. However, I knew I didn't want to do all of those things because A) I didn't like doing all of those things, and B) I wasn't *great* at all of those things.

This is how I decided on the services I was going to offer. First, I researched what other businesses similar to mine were doing and I looked at their service offerings. Second, I began creating a list of which of those services I had both experience in and a desire to do. Finally, I researched how easily accessible these services were for clients. What I mean is, you want to see what kind of competition you have in terms of other software tools, apps, freelancers, as well as other companies that can provide the same service you want to provide. Researching *them* will help you find your unique angle.

For example, there are freelance writers at the ready all over the world. You can find great writers in virtually any industry. How were my writing services going to stand above *and* be more expensive? I decided I would not just be a content writing marketing agency. I needed to connect that writing to marketing and sales. Thus, I turned my writing service into strategy. Yes, I could help you write that social media post, but not only that, I was going to provide the digital know-how to ensure your content was reaching your ideal clients and driving them to action. From this, I even developed my mission statement: "We don't just use pretty words. We use pretty words that work."

Be Liberal with Your Services (At First)

Note this: In the first year of owning your business, you are likely going to have to do some things you have experience with but do *not* enjoy. For me, that was setting up direct mail campaigns and managing logo designs. But remember: It's only temporary. Also, the more you try out different services, or at least offer a variety of services to your clients, the more confident you will feel in narrowing it down to what you *truly* want to offer. Throughout this process, you might realize that you don't want to provide X service or Y service. Guess what? You don't have to.

Substance Over Flash

Once you've decided on your service or product, you need to remember that quality is what matters. Yes, branding your business well is important (more on that in Chapter 4), but quality is *most* important.

In the past, I found that if a client was dragging out the design process because we hadn't landed on the "right shade of pink," for their logo, they weren't ready to own a business. The essence of your brand is beyond the logo. It's a start. It's a hook. You can have all the pretty "things" like sleek business cards, a website with high-quality videos, and a logo that is beyond cool. But if you have nothing beneath that, you're only going to last for a short while.

It's like when a new restaurant opens up in a big city. It's new, exciting, and maybe it checks all the boxes in terms of getting clients in the door. If the service is bad and the food sucks, though, no amount of cool marketing is going to save it in the long run. Consider your business in this same way. You need to focus on the service or product you are delivering above anything else.

> **In simplest terms:**
> A bad logo + great service/product = a successful business
> A great logo + bad service/product = an unsuccessful business

Here is the lesson: All of the marketing and graphic design dollars in the world are not going to create a successful business. Yes, they'll help, but you need to have the bones of a lucrative business first and foremost. This might seem like common sense, but I have seen one too many entrepreneurs become hung up on their logo design for months. That logo wasn't going to make or break their business. Not giving people business cards because their logo wasn't complete – might have.

Pricing Your Services

Once you've decided on your services, you'll want to think about how you're going to price them. Here's a way you can find out how much to charge for your services:

1. Talk to a business coach or consultant: I've mentioned working with a business coach or consultant before because I know the value of having one. A resource in this area will have an unbiased view of your industry and can give you solid advice on where you should position yourself in the market.

2. Research what your job would make in a corporate setting: If what you do is a position in Corporate America, or something close to it, research the salary. The internet will likely give you a range but lean on the higher end of that salary. Remember that your clients are not paying you benefits or paying payroll tax, but you will need to account for taxes on your end as a vendor or subcontractor. You need to keep that in mind when you're setting your rate.

3. Ask others: I know, asking people *what they make* is tacky. However, asking them *what they charge* their clients is perfectly acceptable and helpful. This information gives you a data point on where your own prices fall. I'm forever grateful to the women in my circle who have been forthcoming with what they charge. It informs me whether my rate is standard within my industry while remaining competitive. (Side note: It also helps *all* women remain competitive when we are open about our value.)

How to Develop Your Business Strategy

Another important element of marketing is how your product and cost factor into your brand. Think about your business strategy as a triangle, with three points:

1. The quality of the work you deliver [Product/ Service]
2. The value of the work you produce [Cost]
3. Your ability to meet deadlines and keep a project on track [Delivery]

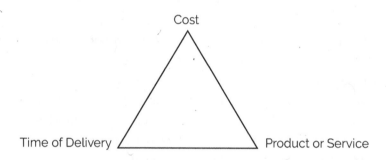

Cost

Time of Delivery

Product or Service

> **A business coach summed it up for me this way:**
> You can have a product that is fast and cheap, **but it won't be good.**
>
> You can have a product that is good and cheap, **but it won't be fast.**
>
> You can have a product that is fast and good, **but it won't be cheap.**

Especially as a new business owner, you won't be able to provide all of these services nor should you be expected to (more on difficult clients later). However, decide where you want to fall in terms of your product/service deliverable. Start with one of these triangular points: Product/ Service, Cost, or Delivery. Once you choose one point, pick the other. From there, you can't be the third.

For example, I'm a fast writer and editor. It doesn't take me much time to read a client's blog and make edits, so for a while I didn't charge for that time. Why would I charge for ten to fifteen minutes? But ten minutes here and there add up, and my business coach reminded me that I shouldn't penalize myself for being quick. In fact, I went to school for three years beyond my under-graduate degree in order to gain more experience in writing and editing. Then I went on to read hundreds (maybe a thousand...) student papers that required editing. All of that expertise made me better at my job. I should not be giving away that service for free. In fact, clients should have been paying me *more* because I worked so quickly and provided high-value results. That's when I determined that my business strategy was **quick** and **good**, but it was not cheap.

Your (Soon-to-Be) Clients

Once you know what service(s) you're offering, you need to know who your ideal client is. Most importantly, you need to *understand* your ideal client. Your ideal client is the dream client. Your services fit a specific need for them. They pay you on time. Together, you build great results. Long story short: You simply enjoy working with them and you make money while doing it.

Everyone has their own definition of what an idea client is, and you, too, will soon have your own definition. However, here is a list of general characteristics that will likely describe an ideal client. This person:

- ✓ Asks good questions
- ✓ Is responsive to phone calls and emails
- ✓ Meets deadlines, when needed
- ✓ Pays on time
- ✓ Is respectful and generally pleasant

Although these are general actions that you are looking for in an ideal client, there are also very specific demographic traits that you will want to consider. These will be unique to your services. For example, my ideal client is a male business owner, white collar, usually in his fifties, with children (usually a daughter), who is beginning to think about retirement. But that may be far from your ideal client. This is where a client avatar is very handy. It will give you a 360-degree view of the person you are trying to land as your client and the more specific you can be, the more easily you can go looking for them.

Because it's so important, I'm going to include this exercise on knowing who your ideal client is here instead of making you wait until the End-of-Chapter Check-In. That's how strongly I feel about it. You can't guess at who your ideal client is. You need to know. This may seem like a waste of time or like it's unnecessary for your industry, but the more you are open to physically writing down the details you're looking for in an ideal client, the quicker they will reveal themselves to you. (Seriously.)

Some people get really specific with their client profiles, to the point where they've basically created a made-up person right down to their shoe size. But especially in your first year of business, you can't expect that your ideal clients are going to fit this mold. In fact, you will likely begin with one client avatar and then shift to a completely different avatar within a few months. I'm still doing that to this day. Any good business should.

You can get more specific later, but for now, answer these questions about your ideal client:

1. Is your ideal client based on gender? If so, why? If not, why?

2. Is your ideal client based on age? If so, why? If not, why?

3. For B2B business leaders: Are you industry-specific? Why?
   Note: B2B means your business is selling directly to another business. For example, you are providing bookkeeping services to restaurants.

4. For B2C business leaders: Are you product-specific? Why?
   Note: B2C means your business is selling directly to consumers. For example, you are creating a board game that will be sold directly to parents of young children.

5. For B2B: What are other characteristics that signal an ideal client? *(Examples: zip code, brick and mortar, completely virtual, influential human resources department, and so on.)*

6. For B2C: Where do your clients shop? In-store? Online? Hybrid?

7. For B2B: How "big" or "old" does this client need to be? Look at the age of the company, the number of employees, and your client's revenue/sales.

8. For B2B and B2C: Which social media channels are your clients most active on?

A lot of valuable information will come from this exercise, but the two things you really want to know are:

- Who is the decision maker?
- How can you speak their language?

Speaking your ideal client's language is a really important skill. It may sound like common sense, but I've seen a lot of entrepreneurs fail to do this: Speak to their audience. Know what their pain point is. Focus on them, not you. Basic sales training dictates that if you're doing most of the talking in the conversation, it's not going well. Ask questions. Be inquisitive. They have a problem. You have a solution. Your solution is your service offering.

In Chapter 4, we'll discuss how to reach your ideal client in depth, so consider this stage of your business-building as a fact-finding mission. You want to get as much information as you can about your potential client so that you know *all* the possible opportunities for you to solve their problem with your service or product. This data will not only influence your marketing later, but it could influence the type of services/products you provide and even naming your business.

Naming Your Business

Once you've decided on what services you're offering and who your ideal client is, you'll be ready to name your business.

When I was first starting my business, I had to think about this, too. Between my friend who was an entrepreneur and my dad who knew me better than anyone – I wasn't sure where to start. At first, I was thinking of naming my business Maximus Marketing, after my dog. This is what they had to say about that idea:

Friend: *Do not name your business after your dog.*

Dad: *I really like that name for your business.*

Great. Very helpful. So, I went back to the drawing board. I eventually circled around to my favorite hobby: writing. Not only did I enjoy writing personally and professionally, it seemed like a safe topic that would explain what my business did without alienating anyone who might find it hard to pronounce my last name. I liked *First Story Marketing*, but that was taken by a marketing agency out West. So, I did what most entrepreneurs do when they find out their awesome name idea already exists: I sulked and then convinced myself it wasn't a great name to begin with. (Now, I can honestly say, I'm glad I didn't go with that name because it sounds too limiting to me. Just the First Story? What comes after?) Eventually, after multiple rounds of scribbling down names and asking for input from those I trusted, I landed on: Next Page Brand Strategies.

We'll cover a bit more on branding and reaching out to your ideal client in Chapter 4, but it's important to think about how your name – the introduction to your brand – exists in relation to what you're offering and who your ideal client is.

While you're thinking of business names, consider what will set you apart from the competition. Look at others in your industry – do you see a theme? Is your name catchy and meaningful and something that people will remember? And, of course, you always have the option of going old-school and looking up Greek words, Roman gods, or Arabic names that will give you a sense of purpose while also sounding very cool.

But if you're really stuck, I honestly don't see any reason why you can't name your business after your dog.

BOOKKEEPING 101

In the last chapter, we covered how important it is to create a budget for yourself, so you can have the right amount saved before starting your business and so you can plan your expenses during that first year. Once you've done that, you also need to think about other finance-related issues. Otherwise, the following might happen:

Three years into running my business, I made a huge mistake when filing taxes as a business owner. Even though I'd filed business taxes before, this was the first time I'd hired 1099 workers, so the tax process would be different for me than in prior years. For context, 1099 workers are contract workers you pay for the work they provide. They are not on a salary and do not receive benefits. There are many nuances to this, but the basic thing to know is that, as a business owner, you do not withhold income tax or pay FICA tax the way you would with a traditional employee. However, you do need to submit information to the government that demonstrates how much you paid these 1099 workers by January 31 of the following year. For example, if you hired contract employees for work in 2019, you would need to submit their 1099s by January 31, 2020.

It wasn't until the first week of February, when I overheard a few others in my coworking space discussing their 1099 workers and what a pain it was to get all of that information to the government, that I knew I was missing something. Wait. What information? Sent to whom? I asked an entrepreneur friend when the deadline was, and she answered: "January 31." And what if I hadn't done it? "You'll be fined," she replied.

Son of a...

I began scrambling and emailing my accountant, including many exclamation points in every subject line. My always-ahead-of-the-deadline self would now be receiving a fine for submitting my 1099s late, so I had to have my accounting books cleaned up for real, versus me anecdotally saying, "Well, I know I paid her over $300 – does that help?"

I'm a smart woman, but the financial organization of my business is *not* my strong suit. I firmly believe that marketing and sales are an important part of your business, but finance/accounting has to be next. I'm a rock star at the former – and a self-proclaimed disaster at the latter. The fact is, when it comes to managing your finances, it either comes naturally or it doesn't. It doesn't, to me. In my first year of business, I knew that more money was better than less money, but other than that, I really didn't know what I was looking at when I opened my bookkeeping software.

And even though I quickly improved at many of the basic elements needed for running a business within my first year – networking, for example – one thing that I *didn't* improve on was finances. I had no financial sense at all. I hated looking at my QuickBooks. I asked, bribed with bottles of wine, and begged anyone I came across who had even some bookkeeping experience to help me. "What are undeposited funds?" I would ask. "Why are numbers in my bank account not matching?" "I know I deposited that check, so why isn't it listed in here?" When I was having coffee with an accountant, just as part of my general networking, she casually mentioned "reconcile my books," and she made it sound very important. As soon as I got back into my car, I frantically Googled the phrase. *What is this, and how do I do it?*

Most small business owners run into a cash flow problem because they aren't getting their finances in order correctly. They're hustling every month trying to pay bills, taking whatever work they can get, undercutting their value, or, worse, working for free. My first year of business, I brought in more than $40,000, and I was pretty excited about that. That was the number I had been pushing toward because that's how much my income had been before I quit my day job. But I had a lot of business and basic living expenses. At the end of the year, I had kept just under $20,000. That was not an income I could live on.

That's why it's so important to get your finances in order as early as possible. By doing this and turning to people who are professionals in this field when needed, you'll be positioning yourself for success.

How to Get Your Finances in Order

I put together this section of the book with the help of my friend and fellow entrepreneur Danielle Kleinrichert, who owns a virtual bookkeeping firm. According to her, it's important for small business owners to:

1. Invoice promptly
2. Reconcile accounts monthly
3. Run reports

Maybe some of these phrases sound familiar to you. Maybe you already know how to do all of these things. Great! Then you can skip this section. However, if you're like me, here's a layman's breakdown of what you should be doing to get your finances in order. And if you can't do it, then find someone who can.

Invoice Promptly

If you can get the money up front, awesome. Even fifty per cent is better than nothing. But, if that's not possible, then you'll want to invoice immediately after the project is completed. Like, within the same hour. The sooner you get that invoice to your client, the sooner you will get paid.

Reconcile Accounts Monthly

There's that word, "reconcile," again. It must be important, huh? You bet. Reconciling keeps your numbers organized. You know how much is coming in and how much is going out while ensuring this is all lined up with your actual bank accounts. For example, let's say you earned $1,000 in the month of January but had $700 in expenses, including coffees, utilities for the business, and payment for the software you need to use to complete your work for clients. That means you made $300 in January. All of those numbers should line up when you look at your accounts as a whole.

Run Reports

You know your numbers by running reports. That $300 I mentioned above? That's a profit, and if that's not the magical number you were hoping to make, you need to establish a plan to bring in more money and spend less. Sounds simple, right? You'd be amazed how hard that is when you're hustling. Running reports will give you hard data points on the "health" of your business. In other words, reports will tell you if you are making money – or not.

Once I understood these concepts better (with some help from Danielle), the math began to make sense. So, I started working in doubles. If I wanted to double what I brought in for year two, then I would double my rate. That was the goal, anyway. Because I couldn't be sure how much time it would take me to complete a project (that was still a learning process), but I would at least start a project with a higher hourly rate. Then, if a project took longer than expected, I might be making less than that amount per hour, but at least I had started at a higher amount to begin with. By the end of my second year, I had brought in close to $88,000. After taxes, business expenses and contributing to my health insurance and retirement, my final "take home" pay was $44,000. That was double what I brought home the year before. Win!

This just goes to show why you need to get your finances in order. If you're not looking at your numbers, then you're "shooting from the hip," as Danielle would say. Without organizing your numbers, you're merely guessing at how much you're making and how much you should charge. Guessing won't keep your business afloat.

HOW TO ASK FOR ADDITIONAL HELP

You will need help in some areas of your business during your first year, and there is nothing shameful in asking for it. In fact, Danielle wasn't the only person I got help from. Throughout the years I've spent running my business, I've learned to ask for help sooner rather than later. Sometimes, this meant getting help from family and friends. I did this a lot when I first started out: when I was coming up with the right name for my business, when I was figuring out how much to charge for my services, when I was learning how to deal with clients, etc. But I often got a lot of different opinions, which meant that I would end up even more confused than before.

Remember when I asked my friend and Dad for advice on whether I should name my business Maximus Marketing? Well, they had opinions on other elements of my business, too.

On How Much to Charge:

Friend: I think if you charge $35 an hour, that's reasonable for what you do.

Dad: You shouldn't be charging less than $150 an hour with your education and background.

On Difficult Clients:

Friend: I would just ignore her comment. Maybe she's having a bad day. I've had clients lose their crap on me, too, and then apologize later.

Dad: Here's what you say: "Screw (he might have used a different expletive here) you, it was nice doing business with you." Then, you hang up the phone.

(Side note: My friend was right on this last one; the client did apologize to me later.)

I needed opinions and I needed support, but getting advice from my friend and my dad didn't always help me. And, unfortunately, typing "I own a marketing agency, how much do I charge?" into Google was also not helping. What I needed was an unbiased third party. That's when I decided to work with a business coach. He landed (not surprisingly) somewhere in the middle of what my friends and family had told me to charge, but he also always pushed me to charge a little more and to remember my worth. As much as it sounded amazing to charge $100 an hour, I just could not do it at first – so I landed on $75. A few months later, as I became busier, he suggested I bump up my rate again. A few months after that, he told me to raise my prices a third time. "Now you're in a competitive place," he said. "You should have been charging this much to begin with."

I hadn't been charging that much before because, well, it sounded insane. Eventually, though, the more people I met, the more networking I did, and the more proposal bids I slung out into the universe, the more I realized that what I was charging – for my type of service – was the industry standard.

I understand how uncomfortable it is for most people, especially women, to talk about how much they make or ask for "a lot" of money. But know this – you are worth it. By arming yourself with the knowledge and data of what others – regardless of gender – are making in your industry, and by asking other professionals their advice, you are positioning yourself as a competitive and valuable asset to your future clients. In fact, you may be surprised to learn that your ideal client would prefer to work with you if you charged *more*. What something "costs" speaks to the value of the service or product. We know that's not always the case, but for you and your business? It will absolutely be worth your client's investment.

The People Who Can Help You

After working with my business coach and feeling satisfied that I was charging a fair price and building the foundation of my business, I recognized a new "gap" for me: sales. Gaps are often described in business as places where you are not quite meeting an expected deliverable. That's what happened to me. I wasn't good at it. And I knew I wasn't good at it, because I was taking a lot of meetings and sending a lot of proposals, but not closing enough business to generate the income I wanted.

The next step for me was to hire a coach who worked specifically in sales. Not only did I need someone to coach me through the process, but I also needed someone to encourage my introvert-personality to actually do the damn sales-thing. Once we started working together, we had check-ins every two weeks where she would walk me through my prospect list, asking me if I had called them and where they stood in the process. I couldn't lie to her. (Well, I could, but then why was I paying her to help me?)

On your journey as an entrepreneur, you should consider hiring a business coach, a sales coach, possibly a marketing consultant, and maybe even someone to help you out with IT or accounting. Wherever you might be lacking in skills, it's worth getting the help you need. You owe it to yourself and to your business. Ask yourself in which of these areas you don't feel naturally confident:

Organization – *Do you struggle with managing your time, setting up meetings, or following up with contacts?*

Managing finances – *Are you unsure how to invoice? Do you need help reconciling your accounts every month?*

Establishing business practices – *Do you know if your prices are competitive? Do you have legal documents (contracts, non-disclosures, etc.) in place to protect you/the business when you begin working with a client?*

Marketing your business – *Do you know how to get people to call or email you? Are you familiar with your digital marketing options and other (perhaps less-known) marketing opportunities?*

Closing sales – *Do you get a lot of meetings but don't close enough business? Do you know when to follow up with people without being a pest?*

There will be more at the End-of-Chapter Check-In on the types of people who can help in each of these areas, but for now, consider where your weaknesses may be. Of course, you may feel relatively confident in all of these areas, in which case – great! However, you will still likely need to move some of these tasks off your desk in order to be most effective. Rank which of these are easiest and quickest for you to complete. Then, consider how you can reach out to people, either in your business network, on LinkedIn, or even through trusted Facebook groups, to help you manage the rest.

End-of-Chapter Check-In

EXERCISE 1: DEFINE YOUR BUSINESS
SPEAK YOUR CLIENT'S LANGUAGE

Remember that your clients are interested in *how you can help them*. Yes, they want to know the services that you offer, but your services are a solution. First, they need to know that you understand the problem (i.e. their pain). Ask these questions:

1. What is your client concerned about?
2. What is their business objective? More customers? A better accounting system? A better product?
3. How come they haven't been able to alleviate this problem in the past?

Now, use this information to help define your service offerings and the results you will give your clients. You may even discover a possible business name during this exercise!

EXERCISE 2: BOOKKEEPING 101
GETTING YOUR FINANCES IN ORDER

You're going to need some way to manage your finances. There are online bookkeeping systems that are targeted to small business owners, such as QuickBooks Online, but there are other options as well. If you're especially organized, an Excel spreadsheet may be enough. However, the more sophisticated your business becomes, the more sophisticated your bookkeeping process will need to be.

Here are some options to review.

1. Virtual Bookkeeper (search for this on LinkedIn, in your area)
2. QuickBooks Online
3. Bench.co
4. Pilot Bookkeeping
5. Bark.com

In my experience, most entrepreneurs start with either an Excel spreadsheet or QuickBooks Online. However, if you don't have a strong accounting background (like myself), then you might need to find a Virtual Bookkeeper. Depending on the complexity of the bills you have to pay for your type of business, and the number of clients you have at the onset, another, more sophisticated agency like Pilot or Bench might be your best resource.

EXERCISE 3: HOW TO ASK FOR ADDITIONAL HELP & UNDERSTANDING THE HELP YOU NEED

Know where your weaknesses are. Just as you can find someone to help you with bookkeeping, you can find other support for all areas of your business. I always recommend starting with LinkedIn, as that will connect you with people who are in your area and who are potentially good long-term contacts. Here are some roles you may want to consider searching for when it comes to support:

1. Virtual Assistant – They will help with your calendar, manage meetings, and may also be able to help manage your social media.
2. Business Coach/Consultant – They will help you establish who you are as a business and will likely have the knowledge to provide industry feedback on your services and cost.
3. Marketing Coach/Consultant – They are different to a business coach. A business coach helps you build the foundation of a business, but a marketing coach will help you reach your ideal clients and provide strategies for how to get these contacts into your pipeline.
4. Sales Coach/Consultant – They are different to a business coach and a marketing coach. They will be able to help you set actionable goals for your prospect list and train you in closing sales.

3

Get Yourself in Order

I learned a few years ago that when I work nonstop for days on end, I'm asking for a shut-down – one way or another. Some people can sleep five hours a night, work a full day, take the red eye to the opposite side of the country, and be bright and fresh for a three-day convention. Not this girl.

So, what happens if we can't operate that way, but we don't mind our own limits? Our bodies will come crashing to a halt, as if to say, "You're not going to take a rest? Fine. I'll make you." That's exactly where I ended up one weekend in the fall of 2018 when I over-worked myself. I was trying to self-diagnose (*food poisoning? The flu? The Bubonic plague?*), but it didn't really matter what it was. What mattered was how terrible I was feeling. I didn't have the energy to move beyond my couch, and I felt dizzy if I looked at any screen for longer than two minutes. (Turns out, I found out later, that I was experiencing a debilitating migraine.)

When you're working at a corporate job, you know how this scenario plays out. You're fighting an illness, and you're debating with yourself about whether or not you're going to make that call (or text) to your boss to let them know that you're taking a sick day. So, how do you make that decision for yourself when you're the boss? It might seem easy enough. *I don't have to work tomorrow*, you might say to yourself, *so I'll just take it easy.* But what happens when you have a first-time meeting with a new contact? Rescheduling is okay, but not a great first impression, right? What if you have a major presentation with a potential client that you've been prepping for over the last couple of weeks? What if you're in the middle of providing a strategic plan with a hard deadline?

Well, for starters, you can do what I did. Stop working until you feel better.

But the hard reality is that I didn't learn my lesson. This was only a temporary solution, stopping *after* I was sick. About four months later, I was hit with another two-day migraine. That's when I began scheduling meditation into my calendar. And then, a few months later, that proved still not to be enough: I had three migraines in the span of three weeks. *Okay,* I said to myself, *you have to make your health a priority.* Well, I finally decided to do just that, and completely changed my routine. I began my mornings with yoga or a workout, scheduled lunch breaks that did not involve me standing over my laptop while eating, and began calling it quits by mid-afternoon on Fridays. Soon after that, my migraines dwindled. I was sleeping better, had more energy during the day, and overall felt less anxious and more focused.

For me, migraines were a sign that I was not taking care of myself, because they were triggered by just that. You probably have your own sign that's triggered when you're not in a great place. Physical or emotional, it could be insomnia, racing thoughts, or a stomachache. And if you don't take care of yourself during the first year of your business, these symptoms will happen to you. A lot.

That's why it's so important for you to get yourself in order when you start your business. You need to know yourself – and what you need – to both be healthy *and* run your business efficiently. The last thing you want is to burn out.

> **To get yourself in order, you need to know:**
> 1. The importance of self-care
> 2. How to find your people
> 3. How to navigate the emotional transition of becoming a business owner

THE IMPORTANCE OF SELF-CARE

One time, after a particularly difficult conversation with a client, I ended up sitting in front of my computer crying. She hadn't been respectful of my boundaries (more on this in Chapter 7) and she had made me feel small. I wanted to crawl into bed, pull the sheets over my head, and pretend that there was someone else to deal with my ringing phone. *Why did I sign up for this?* I thought. *This isn't freeing, empowering, or bringing me happiness.*

Of course, not every interaction in your business will be rosy. And when they're not, it's important to take care of yourself so that you don't become burned out from experiencing the negative aspects of the job. I knew this, so after this incident, I decided to do exactly that. I turned off my laptop. I called my mom to vent. I took my dog, Max, for a long walk. When I got back home, I did my laundry, cooked dinner, and took a hot bath. Before going to bed, I had come to the incredibly freeing realization that I wouldn't have to work with this difficult client ever again. She wasn't my boss. She wasn't even a co-worker. I could simply *stop* working with her after our project was complete. That helped me sleep peacefully that night.

Whenever I complain about the weird people I meet in business, my mom often quotes a lyric from The Doors, saying to me with a shrug, "People are strange." Or, another favorite of hers: "They don't get any better when they're my age, Cassandra." Ugh, great. But she and Jim Morrison are both right. People are strange, and a rude person has likely been rude their entire life. It's important to keep some perspective while also managing your own self-care routine.

However, self-care is important in a lot of areas of your business – even if your clients are great (which they often will be). For example, you could be working late nights on a large proposal with a hard deadline. Or you could have a day with a lot of "emergency" requests

THIS WON'T BE PRETTY

and you never even touch your to-do list for the day. Regardless of the cause, it's important to support yourself by practicing self-care. Doing this includes:

1. Listening to your gut (and body)
2. Creating a healthy schedule
3. As my mother would say, "Taking a Mental Health Day"

Listening to Your Gut (And Body)

At the beginning of this chapter, I described the terrible migraines I went through when I was overworking myself. Whatever your own version of this is – increased heart rate, insomnia, racing thoughts, headaches, stomachaches – you need to learn to recognize it. You need to know what happens to your body, physically and emotionally, when you're overworking yourself or feeling stressed, because it's a sign that you need to stop and slow down. I know that in your first year of business, it will seem like you don't have time to do this. That you just can't. And I get that. But there are three significant consequences you'll have to face if you refuse to stop and slow down:

1. You'll get sick
2. You'll be difficult to work with
3. Because of 1 and 2, your business will suffer

So, stop and slow down. Once you've done this, you'll want to do whatever makes you feel whole and gives you energy. It's been trial and error for me, but I've discovered those activities for myself, as I hope you will, too. For me, it's re-watching a favorite episode of a

Netflix show. It's taking my dog, Max, for a walk. It's stretching a bit on my yoga mat, even if I'm not doing a full practice. It's listening to a true crime comedy podcast. It's writing out an angry letter full of what I want to say to someone and then not actually sending it.

Here are some strategies you might want to try when you're having a particularly rough day:

1. Go for a walk while listening to music, a book, or a podcast
2. Burn your favorite candle
3. Sit outside in the sun for ten minutes
4. Work out, getting your heart rate up for at least twenty minutes
5. Stretch (try "Yoga with Adrienne" on YouTube)
6. Pet your dog or cat
7. Watch a funny movie or TV show
8. Write in a journal
9. Take a bath or a hot shower
10. Volunteer with a favorite organization

Creating a Healthy Schedule

It's also important that you create a healthy schedule. In Chapter 1, we went over how to create a schedule that will help you keep yourself organized no matter what you have on your plate. Now, it's time for you to create a schedule that prioritizes your emotional and mental health.

When I started my business, I found that I was always spinning around, bouncing between one project and the next, between one priority and another. It didn't make any sense to me why this was happening. I was someone who had multiple calendars, hardbound and digital. I had multi-colored highlighters and pens, and each color was designated to a certain level of importance. I had program management systems in place that sent me daily reminders of the tasks I had due that day. The point is: Even though I was very organized, I was still low-key anxious all the damn time. I was half-completing requests or working late into the night when my phone was finally quiet and I could actually concentrate.

While some people struggle to stay away from Netflix, laundry, or naps when they're working from home, I'm the opposite. I can't stop working. That sounds like it would make me a successful business owner, but in reality, it set me up for burnout. Sitting at a desk for nine hours straight? Only getting up to use the restroom, refill my water glass, or grab something from the kitchen twenty feet away? Not exactly a break.

None of my previous jobs had ever had that much dedication from me. None.

The danger of burnout meant that I had to commit to changing my schedule so that my anxiety levels would lower. So, I decided to create work hours with an actual lunch break. I'd begin work at 9 a.m., take my lunch break around noon for at least thirty minutes (which was a *true* break: I would walk my dog or watch an episode on Netflix), then call it quits at 6 p.m. This schedule was by no means perfect or absolute, but it was at least a goal to strive for. Without having that goal in mind, I could easily have continued down a path of long, unhealthy days.

As a whole, once I put these parameters around my days, I found I was more conscious on whether I was working too much. *Did I take a lunch break today?* I'd ask myself. If I didn't, I knew I needed to quit work early to take Max for a walk. At first, it felt like I was slacking. I should be hustling 24/7, shouldn't I? But that's what I had done the whole year before. And what also happened that year? I had two massive migraines that sent me to bed for two days straight with nausea and vomiting.

It's a common American mindset that if you are not working yourself to death, you're lazy. Mental, emotional and physical health often takes a backseat to being successful. However, there has thankfully been a shift in the last few years. Employees at large corporate offices are given multiple resources to support their health. Lowe's Corp. here in North Carolina has beautiful walking paths, a Zen garden, and a state-of-the art fitness center for their employees.[2]

True leaders know the benefits of taking care of their own health and, therefore, place a high value on their employees doing the same. Andrew Cherng, the founder of Panda Express, once stopped a meeting and encouraged a manager to meditate in order to reduce his anxiety. He has said that he practices meditation regularly and

---

[2] Wilson , Cristina. "Lowe's HQ Just Opened Their State-of-the-Art Fitness Center on Campus." *Charlotte Agenda*, 16 Jan. 2019, www.charlotteagenda.com/154725/lowes-hq-fitness-mooresville-jobs/.

continuously encourages his staff to invest in self-improvement habits, including meditation and other hobbies that they enjoy. Cherng said in 2008, "You can't expect someone to do a good job if you treat them like an object."[3] Cherng, who helped his father open his first restaurant in 1983, now has over 2,200 locations worldwide and a net worth of $3.5 billion, according to *Forbes*.[4] Proof that you can be successful *and* take care of your health.

What is something that is the opposite of work that you love to do? Paint? Read a book? Work out? Block it off in your calendar. Don't move it for anything. Make this a priority, just as you would a client call or meeting. It's a meeting with yourself, and you are too important to cancel plans with. Set aside at least thirty minutes a day for that activity. If you need to schedule this as part of your lunch break in the middle of the day – perfect. If you can't find time during the day, then make sure it happens before you sit down at your desk, or set a true cut-off time at the end of the day to make sure it happens in the evening.

Taking a Mental Health Day

I've heard the phrase "taking a mental health day" much more recently in casual conversations, and I'm glad of it. Because I've known the importance of mental health days ever since I was a kid.

---

[3] Connley, Courtney. "Marc Benioff, Oprah and 3 Other Business Leaders Say This Habit Is Key to Their Success." *CNBC*, CNBC, 23 June 2018, www.cnbc.com/2018/06/22/marc-benioff-oprah-and-others-say-this-is-key-to-their-success.html.
[4] Carnegie Corporation of New York. "Andrew Cherng." *Carnegie Corporation of New York*, 2019, www.carnegie.org/awards/honoree/andrew-cherng/.

When we were growing up, my mother was very attuned to my sister's and my emotions. We rarely got sick, so "taking a sick day" wasn't common. But that didn't mean that we didn't need a break from school. Every few months, Mom would notice that we were getting burned out or exhausted from school and other social activities. That's when she would ask us if we needed a mental health day. Taking a mental health day meant taking a break from all the to-dos on our list that could wait, including schoolwork. We could sleep in. Lounge around in our pajamas. She might take us out shopping or out to lunch. It helped us reset, and we would reengage fresher and more focused when we returned to school.

There will always be something on your to-do list, and this will never be truer than when you are starting a business. However, it's infinitely important to schedule long breaks, too, so you don't burn yourself out so badly that you become sick (like I did).

Of course, everyone has their own tolerance for stress. Some people may need shorter mental health breaks several times a month while other people can go several months before feeling burned out. I would recommend planning a mental health day at least once a quarter, or once every three months. If you're unsure whether it's time, ask yourself the following:

- Do I feel more agitated than normal?
- Am I making silly mistakes at work?
- Do I have any leftover energy at the end of the day to do things I enjoy?

Take the full day off, if you can. If you can't do that, how about just the afternoon? Can you take a walk at a nearby park? Can you turn off your phone for just a few hours? Sure you can. If you find it difficult to commit to doing this, find a friend who will help keep you accountable and take your mental health days together. Even if s/he is not an entrepreneur, you could both benefit from the break.

I would also recommend scheduling this day off as far in advance as you can, just as you would schedule any vacation time. Block it out on your calendar so you can't schedule any other meetings that day and, if you can, schedule other "self-care" appointments, like a massage or haircut, that you would have to physically cancel if you decide to work that day.

HOW TO FIND YOUR PEOPLE

On my first birthday after I had started my business, a friend of mine wanted to bring over some wine to celebrate. Unfortunately, my birthday fell on a Wednesday.

"Ugh," I said, frowning. "Not tonight. Maybe this weekend."

"What's wrong with tonight?"

"I'm overwhelmed with work," I replied.

I wasn't just overwhelmed. I was on the verge of tears.

When I did see my friend that weekend, not only did she bring a bottle of wine (okay, maybe two), but she also brought two large packs of file folders, a pack of printer paper and – I began jumping for joy when I opened this – a label maker. This time, I was on the verge of tears because of how thoughtful and useful the gift was. My friend wasn't an entrepreneur, so she didn't exactly understand what had been stressful about my week or why I couldn't go out on my actual birthday. But what she did understand was that she could support me by providing supplies. (That label maker, by the way, is still one of my favorite birthday gifts.)

Finding your people – the people who support you – is so important, and it's okay if they're not an entrepreneur like you. What is important is that you know whom you can lean on and how they can help you so that you're back to your confident, happier self sooner rather than later. The process for finding your people is twofold. It requires:

1. Creating your support network
2. Dealing with unsupportive people and setting boundaries

Creating Your Support Network

It's important to find people with diverse backgrounds and opinions to be a part of your support network. Some of these people will be entreprenuers, which will help you feel supported in terms of your business. They will empathize with what you are going through and be able to provide helpful advice, or a safe space for you to feel supported. Others may provide different but equally important kinds of support.

Friends and Family

When building a support network, it's easiest to start with those people you know. Engaging with friends and family who have known you a long time and know the "you" outside of business is important for your mental and emotional health. After all, the person you are at your core won't just dissapear once you become an entreprenuer, so it's important to have people around you who will keep you grounded to your core beliefs and values.

However, it's also important to keep those around you who are supportive and cheerleaders for your business versus the nay-sayers or people who only look at the negative side of things. You may have a friend or family member you are very close to, but if they are not supportive in the way you need when it comes to your business, then it's important to keep them at distance where your business is concerned. We'll discuss specific strategies for navigating this type of realtionship in the next section. For now, just know that including someone in your support network should be earned. Your time and energy are valuable and worth protecting.

Other Entreprenuers

Fellow entrepneruers will be fairly easy to find, esepecially once you begin networking. However, similar to your family and friends, you will want to choose carefully which of these entrepreneurs should be a part of your support network, especially since this should be a two-way street. You should also provide support for them. Some general guidelines for finding the right entreprenurial support network may include:

- People who are on a similar point in their journey to you (i.e. just starting their business)
- People in a similar industry
- People with a similar home life (partner, spouse, kids, no kids, etc.)

Once you hit your first major hurdle of owning a business, or you have your first question that Google can't seem to answer, you'll want to reach out to this network. Every time you mine this network for answers or support, consider how each person responds and whether you are helped, or feel better, after the exchange. If the answer is "no," they can reamin a business contact but they simply don't need to be a part of your support network.

Strategies

Finding your people is just as important as prioritizing your self-care. Especially when you're starting your business, you need to make time for your support network, and expand it if necessary. Here are some strategies you can use to engage with the right people:

1. Schedule a walk-and-talk versus sitting for coffee or talking on the phone
2. Invite them to a webinar or a book club that would be beneficial for you both (even if they are not an entrepreneur, a friend or family member would likely enjoy some professional learning)
3. Celebrate your respective "wins" of the week with a happy hour or dinner

4. Share podcasts or other resources and follow up with a conversation on how you're implementing those strategies in your own lives

5. Schedule a workout time once a week and hold each other accountable

Spend time with the people who love you and support you. People will become closer friends because of their endless support, even if they don't really understand what "being fired by a client" feels like. They just know that you need a laugh and to be yourself for a while.

Remember that it also takes some time to build your support network. It took me a while to find my people, and even now, a few years into it, I still struggle with who my trusted advisors are (and I'm sure that, in another five to ten years, they will be different people again). As you grow and adapt, so should your support network.

Once you've spent some time with these people, put on whatever makes you feel awesome (a blazer, tennis shoes, leopard-print leggings, whatever), and you'll be ready to get back out there and hustle.

Dealing with Unsupportive People and Setting Boundaries

There's going to be more on unsupportive people and boundaries in Chapters 6 and 7, but I wanted to talk here about people in your personal life who might not be supportive of you – or whom you might have to set boundaries with. These people include your friends, family, and anyone who lives with you.

Your Friends

The fact is, the people who are around you will change when you begin this journey. It's a lot like having a baby. If you have a child, you gravitate toward friends who also have children. If you don't have a child, it's natural to spend more time with people who don't have children. This isn't a hard and fast rule, but it tends to work out this way. It's the same with owning a business. When you run your own business, you end up around people who run their own business, too.

Also, like with having a child, there may be people in your life who get tired of your stories. They might be thinking to themselves, *"Can we talk about anything other than their business?"* Sure you can. But if you've had a particularly awesome week, it's all you want to talk about. That's fair. You should. Just remember that not everyone is on the same page. Regardless of that, though, any supportive friend is going to want to hear about your life (even if they can't relate). Unfortunately, there will be people who choose not to be supportive, because of their own insecurities, the fact that they can't adapt to your new relationship, or simply because they're not a great friend. That's fine. Just make sure they aren't a part of your sacred and safe support network.

Keep in mind that friendship, like any relationship, is a two-way street. You have to be supportive, too. It's on you to explain your new life to the people you care about. I didn't realize it, but when I started my business, I was terrible at getting back to my friends when they texted me. Back when I had a salaried job, I would respond fairly quickly as long as I wasn't in a meeting. At some point after starting my business, I realized that I would read a message, think about my response, but never actually respond. Weeks would go by and a friend might reach out again with, "Hey… uh, I guess you're busy?" because it was so unlike me not to reply on the same day I'd received their text.

The thing was, I was busy. But that wasn't an excuse. I needed to reset the expectations for how my days looked now. I also had to speak to a few friends about establishing what this new world looked like for me. "Please don't be offended if I don't respond to you right away," I would say. "Ask me again in a couple of days if you haven't heard from me. I swear it's not personal!" (And it wasn't.) Or "I have no money to go out, and I'm stressed all the time. Can we just stay in and chill, please?"

The friends who got it stayed. And those who didn't faded into the sunset. And that's okay, because you need cheerleaders in your life no matter what. This entrepreneurial journey can be a lonely one, so you don't need anyone else making you feel more alienated than you already do.

Your Family

You may be one of those lucky few whose parent is an entrepreneur, which means that you have their support (or at least their empathy). For many of us, though, this is new, unchartered territory. Often, being the family's first business owner requires sitting down with a parent and inviting them to have a frank and honest conversation with you.

For me, it was twofold. With my mom, I needed to explain that I was in the office between the hours of 9 a.m. and 6 p.m., even if I was sitting on my couch with my laptop.

"I know, but we could always go take a break and run to the mall," she said.

"Unless we can do it an hour, it's not happening," I replied, knowing full well that no shopping trip with my mom has ever lasted less than three and a half hours.

With my dad, I had to reframe business questions for him.

"Dad, I have a question."

"Sure, sweetie."

"Okay, but I need you to talk to me like a business colleague and not your daughter."

He would laugh and then say, "Okay, Cassandra. What's going on?"

I also had some issues with my family when I was thinking of starting my business, because it was the first time a woman in our family had considered doing so. Because I was a woman taking on a business of my own with literally nothing but my own willpower and grit, my plan to become an entrepreneur was perceived as an unnecessary risk by my old-school Italian American family.

When I was weighing the options of either applying for a leadership position at another non-profit or starting my own business, I remember what my father said to me:

"If you were married, it would be a much easier decision to start a business. Then you would have the support."

"Or," I replied, "it's better that I don't have a family, because if I fail, it will only affect me."

My father, not one to agree easily, replied with, "Yes, but you would at least be on someone else's insurance."

My rebuttal: "I can always get my own health insurance. I don't think it's that hard." (It wasn't.)

The reality is that there is no one perfect time to start a business. Family or not. Married or single. It's all a gamble, as are most big decisions in life.

While dealing with these issues with my family, I learned quickly that my story was not unique. In fact, there was some solidarity in facing this challenge. Women older and younger than me have had to fight this uphill battle within their own support networks. Their family and friends thought it wasn't worth taking the risk. But then, with that logic – why do anything when there's a chance you might fail? Why get married? Why go to school? Why leave the house, even? Every choice has the potential for failure. So, you might as well stick to your guns and run your own business, even if you're the first woman in your family to do so.

Eventually, having my own business made the relationship I had with my dad stronger. He may not have been comfortable with me taking this risk on my own, but once I had made the decision and moved forward, he ensured that I remained all-in. Whenever I was dealing with any of the biggest struggles that plague new entrepreneurs – time management, no boundaries with clients, inconsistent income – I would call him to ask for help. At first, I was afraid that his advice might turn into a lecture (as fathers are accustomed to giving), but, instead, he would lay out actionable strategies that I needed to consider for each hurdle I was facing. As my business grew, he continued to give me advice. This was especially helpful when I started having experiences similar to his from when he'd been working in sales and holding leadership positions as a vice president, board member, and beyond.

I recognize that I am very fortunate to have a parent who made the shift from being cautious and (what I felt was) unsupportive to being one of my most trusted business advisors. Not everyone in your life will do that for you, and it's probably not because they don't want to support you, but because they don't understand what you need. Some of this you can control, but a lot of it you can't. At the end of this section on dealing with unsupportive people and setting boundaries, I'll provide some strategies to help you control what you can.

The People You Live With

Starting a business does not yield immediate results, and anyone living in your space will be the first to witness this. Especially in the beginning, you may be on your laptop or phone all the time, yet, you haven't signed a client yet. Even though they theoretically know you're working, they might begin to ask questions about house chores that you should be doing or errands that you could accomplish. After all, they might reason, since you "own" your schedule unlike other people, you have the time. But this is not the case; you *are* working, so you don't have the time. Because they might not understand this, I highly recommend setting realistic expectations for the people you share your living space with.

If you have a partner, it's important that they be supportive. It's hugely important – in fact, one of the big problems in my marriage that led to my divorce was a lack of support for my career. When I was starting my business, I realized quickly that my home life when I'd been married would have made it impossible for me to run my business, or at least nearly impossible. Certainly, it would have been impossible for me to run it successfully. I still think about that to this day.

What happens if you don't have a supportive partner? Well, here's what happened to me:

When I got married, I was an adjunct professor still in graduate school. My paycheck was barely covering the cost of gas to get me to campus three days a week. Six months after we were married, I mentioned getting my Ph.D. to my husband because I was thinking of moving up the higher education ladder. As you can tell from the lack of "Dr." in front of my name on this book cover, that conversation did not go in my favor. So, I settled into my work as an adjunct professor, believing that, with enough hard work, the opportunity would arise to secure a full-time position.

By the summer of 2015, I had become exhausted – physically and emotionally – because of my adjunct work. So, I considered going back to marketing, which was my first job out of undergrad. This industry, which included a combination of my salary and the educational support from the corporate office, had paid for my graduate studies and was, therefore, very meaningful to me. Plus, I enjoyed it and felt like there always something new to learn when the marketing landscape changed so quickly day to day. I was rarely bored.

To prepare myself for this career move, I checked out *Lean In* by Sheryl Sandberg from the local library. Sandberg wrote about the importance of having a supportive partner. If women are to be successful, she argued, especially if they are married and more so if they are married with children, they need to be in a position where they are supported to chase their dream. Dad is helping out more with the kids. Everyone is splitting the chores. When responsibilities are shared, Mom then has time to reach her own goals. That's when I realized that I hadn't just "unconsciously" put my goals on the backburner; I was not in a relationship that would cultivate the space for me to achieve them.

When my ex and I divorced, I had a new list of what I was looking for in a partner. Naturally, with experience comes wisdom, and I was going to be very particular about who was a part of my story going forward. A big requirement: shared support for both of our careers. Looking back, there are many reasons why I'm glad I'm not married to my ex-husband anymore, but one of the big ones is that, in my new situation, it's possible for me to run my own business. I know that if I were still in that relationship, I would never have had the support at home to make that dream possible.

From this experience, I learned that it was very important whom I had beside me while I was achieving my dreams. This is important no matter your gender, but historically speaking, women tend to take on this supportive role while men are the bread winners. So, what happens if *both* are the bread winners, or just the woman is? In my experience, it's important to have the right kind of partner who is willing and able to take on more responsibility at any given time. This might just be for a few hours, or it might be a few months. I've learned that someone ready and willing to jump in and do this in our relationship (business related or not) is the kind of partner that I can grow with without sacrificing my dreams and goals.

Strategies

The people who love you want to be supportive – they just might not know how to be. Luckily, you can help these people help you. There's a great quote I'm reminded of that states, "Boundaries don't keep people out; they just show people where the door is."

Below, you can check out the strategies I've used for setting boundaries with the people who love me as well as showing them how they can support me. By using these strategies yourself, you can help your family, friends, and the people who live with you understand how to be a part of your support network in a way that is meaningful for everyone involved:

1. Set up regular "check-in" times such as coffee, lunch, or a drink after work. Even if it's once a quarter – get something on the calendar so the people that are important to you feel seen.

2. Create boundaries at home. This one can be especially hard if you're both entrepreneurs. I have dated an entrepreneur, so I know that creating these boundaries can be especially tough. However, for me, I cannot (and do not want to) discuss work every minute of the day. Create rules around no cell phone/laptop zones – for instance, not at the kitchen table or in the bedroom.

3. Be sure to surround yourself with other entrepreneurs. You are not alone in the struggles you're facing, and it's important to seek out peers who can be a sounding board for all aspects of your life. This also helps to keep you from seeking support from friends and/or family who may not feel qualified.

4. Test the water. Whether you're talking to a friend or a family member, share with them the high points of what's going on at work. This will open the door for a deeper conversation, without putting the pressure on them to respond "correctly" to any issues you're facing.

5. Don't respond. If someone is unsupportive or is draining your energy, you don't need to respond to their text, email, or call. Set it aside for now until you're able to respond to them with focus and clarity.

HOW TO NAVIGATE THE TRANSITION OF BECOMING A BUSINESS OWNER

Finally, it's important for you to understand that there's an emotional transition that happens when you become a business owner.

It will be easy to feel defeated during your first several months of business. The only other level of stress that I can compare it to is going through a really bad breakup. You could say that you *are* breaking up with your former life, because you are. You'll find yourself bouncing like a pinball between elation and depression, from signing your first client to firing your first client (and, honestly, they may be the same person). There will be mornings when you wake up and think, "I would love to go sit in a cubicle today and not have to *think* about where my next paycheck is coming from." Just as you pine for an ex you know deep down was never good for you, you'll occasionally do the same with your old life. It's natural. We do this because we crave familiarity. But I promise, leaving that old life – just like leaving an ex – will make you much happier in the long run.

You also might feel scared. And that's normal, too. Three weeks before I quit my job with the plan to start my own business, I wrote in my blog: "I am leaving a stable job for insecurity. I am taking a risk that I never [would have] thought I was capable of." I thought if I typed those words it would make me feel braver. It did not.

But I had to go for it. Transitions are a part of life. We know this. Just as fall has to pass so that winter can be born, just as spring has to end to give birth to summer. But we still want to rush through it. Make things "normal" again. Find a balance. The in-between-ness is too raw. It shows us who we are, and sometimes that's not a pretty picture. We could argue that we aren't ourselves during transitional periods, that we're "just really stressed right now," and that, when they're over, we'll finally be whole again. Yet, what if this time – the time we're always rushing to get through – is actually the best part? Uncomfortable? Yes. Scary? Sure. Necessary? Absolutely. Too many of us (myself included) rush the transition. It's not a fun place to be. We don't know how we're going to feel from one moment to the next. In the morning, we may feel optimistic and happy about this new change, but by mid-afternoon, we're questioning the entire existence of the universe. But without this transition, there is no change. And knowing it's a part of every entrepreneur's journey brings with it a sense of peace and comfort.

Everything will change in your life when you become a business owner: literally, figuratively, metaphorically, emotionally, spiritually, and mentally. Every cell of your being and the surrounding four-mile radius is going to be affected by this new transition. This includes your relationships, friends, pets, and home. You'll probably experience an emotional breakdown more than once, thinking to yourself, *What the hell am I doing? I have made a giant mistake.*

All normal. And, by the way, not knowing what you're doing is part of it. (And, no, you haven't made a giant mistake.)

You should also know that the life of an entrepreneur can be a lonely one. There are decades of studies which show that all animals survive and thrive best within a community. Humans are no different. Relational support is viewed by psychologists as having a long-term effect on thriving.[5] You may feel lonely, now that you aren't on a "team" in the workforce, and you'll wish you were sharing this responsibility with someone else. But, for right now, it's on you.

Strategies

The most important thing to do while going through this transition is not fight it. This transition will happen no matter what when you're becoming an entrepreneur (or taking on *any* new life role), and the more you fight it, the more painful it will be. I could add in a metaphor about the caterpillar transitioning into a butterfly, but you get the gist. Don't fight against your transition; accept it. Here are some strategies to help make it a little easier:

Create a support network of other entrepreneurs – these can be people in your hometown or even across the country. Both virtual

---

[5] Feeney, Brooke C, and Nancy L Collins. "A New Look at Social Support: a Theoretical Perspective on Thriving through Relationships." *Personality and Social Psychology Review: an Official Journal of the Society for Personality and Social Psychology, Inc*, U.S. National Library of Medicine, May 2015. www.ncbi.nlm.nih.gov/pmc/articles/PMC5480897/. .

and in-person entrepreneur groups can provide the support you need.

Talk to others who have been where you now are. I still do this one. As you meet more people, you'll find individuals who have gone through the same struggles you have and can empathize. Ask them for mentorship. Listen when they speak.

Immerse yourself in your new role via books, podcasts, documentaries, and so on. It doesn't matter what industry they're on; when you become an entrepreneur, you're walking the same path as many, many women and men before you, even if their industry is different to yours. Read what they have written. Listen to what they've said. Watch their stories. This will create a sense of normalcy for what you're experiencing, so the transition will feel less foreign.

End-of-Chapter Check-In

EXERCISE 1: SELF-CARE

There's a chance that you've never even thought about a real "mental health day" or day off – no matter what type of work you are in. Especially for women, and I know it's the case for me, it's easy to feel guilty about disconnecting from real life.

If it's difficult for you to take a day off or give yourself a mental health day, try to view yourself in this exercise the same way my mom viewed my sister and me: as children. Think of yourself as a child, and think about how you would treat your eight, ten, or thirteen-year-old self if they were feeling completely overwhelmed by school and/ or life. What would you say? What would you recommend to them/encourage them to do on their day off? Here are some ideas:

- An activity that gets your heart rate up
- An activity that does not include looking at a screen
- An activity where you use your hands

If you can't do any of the above because you don't feel comfortable disconnecting from work during the week, even for an hour, consider how you can do some good for yourself while still being productive. Some ideas:

- Schedule calls or meetings that can be done while walking outside.
- Do chair exercises or chair yoga while you're listening to/watching a webinar.
- Look at your network. Maybe there's someone that you'd like to get to know better. See if you have a shared hobby: Pilates, yoga, or even attending workshops on improving your business. Invite them to join you.

EXERCISE 2: HOW TO FIND YOUR PEOPLE

Who are the people you stay connected with through your phone (via text or social media messaging)? Give them a heads up on your new work schedule/work life. Tell them what you need from them.

Consider the people you live with, or who are close to you – children, parents, siblings, your significant other, and anyone else that you have a close relationship with. Look at each relationship separately. How will you set real-istic boundaries? Fill out the chart on the following page to answer this question.

Person/Relationship	Boundary Needed
Example: Partner or Roommate	Home chores are still a shared responsibility and should not be done during business hours.

EXERCISE 3: HOW TO NAVIGATE THE TRANSITION OF BECOMING A BUSINESS OWNER

It's important to remember that others have been where you are. By meeting some of these people and gathering a list of resources related to the journeys of entrepreneurs like yourself, this new, unfamiliar world will feel less foreign to you. Here's how to do it:

1. Who are three people in your network who are also starting a business? Schedule regular coffees or check-ins with them to share battle stories.
2. Find one to two people who are in your industry but ahead of you in business by five to ten years. Ask them for coffee. Learn their stories.
3. Find physical/digital resources in the following categories:
   a. Memoirs/books on leadership/entrepreneurship
   b. Podcasts about your industry/entrepreneurship/ leadership
   c. Documentaries about your industry/entrepreneurs/ possibly sports legends that have overcome great hurdles

Get Your Business Out There

There are a lot of ways to get your business out into the universe. There's posting on social media, mailing postcards to a potential client list, or inflating those neon, orange, blow-up air dancers and putting them out in front of your building. When it came to getting my business out there, I leaned into my skillset and what brought me comfort: writing. This was a win-win for me. Writing gave me a safe space to process the transition of becoming a new business owner, *and* it helped me create marketing content that kept my name – and my business's name – in front of people.

Blogging, much like any type of marketing, requires consistency and purpose. You have to keep at it before you see results, and you have to know why you're doing it. For my marketing company, I posted two times a week. In terms of purpose, I wanted to show people that my brand was A) knowledgeable (twenty per cent of my blog posts were about social media "how-to" or news) and B) relatable. As a small business owner working with other small business owners, having relatable content was incredibly important, because it made my business stand out from other marketing companies. I understood what my clients' pains were because I'd been there, too.

When I posted my blogs, I would then share them on all of my social media channels and in my e-newsletter. It wasn't until eight or nine months after I'd started that I began getting feedback from people in my network. "I really loved your post last week," they would say. Or "I always look forward to reading your blogs." These blog posts were also easily shareable content that my network could pass on to their networks as an example of my work and knowledge.

By the end of my first year in business, I had several people in my network who I wasn't actively chasing who would call me and say, "I've been reading your blogs. I really connected with your writing. Can we talk about how you can help with my branding?"

Never underestimate the power of cultivating your unique talents to connect with future clients. Furthermore, no matter what you choose to share, keep in mind that you have to share it as often as possible. A couple social media posts every few months won't cut it. One amazing video will have a shelf life, too. By having a strong online presence, you'll make your business known and connect with potential clients and partners. No matter your industry, or your comfort level with digital marketing, your audience is online. In 2020, there were 3.96 billion social media users worldwide. Or fifty-one per cent of the world's total population.[6] According to that same report in August 2020, between 2019 and 2020 there have been roughly more than 376 million new users who have joined a social media platform, or twelve new users every *second*.

More importantly, however, users are not flocking to social media platforms simply to view funny cat videos or "like" photos of their best friend's sorority sister's wedding. Users are, in fact, more active on these platforms when it comes to A) receiving important news and information and B) learning more about a product or service they want to purchase. When the COVID-19 pandemic began in early 2020, social media usage increased significantly. The result of lockdowns and quarantine forced people to take more action via their digital resources. Currently, "social networks are now the second most popular destination for internet users looking for information about brands."[7] (The first? Google.)

> ## To get your business out there, you'll need to understand:
>
> 1. Branding 101
> 2. How to reach your ideal client
> 3. How to write the right content
> 4. How to build a connection

[6] Kemp, Simon. "More Than Half of the People on Earth Now Use Social Media." *Hootsuite*, 19 Aug. 2020, blog.hootsuite.com/simon-kemp-social-media/.
[7] Kemp, Simon. "More Than Half of the People on Earth Now Use Social Media." *Hootsuite*, 19 Aug. 2020, blog.hootsuite.com/simon-kemp-social-media/.

BRANDING 101

When I think about business branding, I'm reminded of the old Beatles song "With a Little Help from My Friends."

One way or another, you're on a stage when you're an entrepreneur. You have to get your name and business out there, but, unlike The Beatles, you're a one-person b(r)and. So, the simpler and more approachable your brand is (I'll discuss how a brand is approachable later), the easier it will be for your friends, family and other network partners to help share your business with their networks.

Your brand represents every aspect of your business. Your brand includes how people feel when they do business with you, the type of packaging that your product comes in, and even how you/your employees answer the phone. Some elements of your brand are tangible, but many parts are not. The founder of Amazon, Jeff Bezos (love him or hate him, he's still an entrepreneur), said it best: "Your brand is what people say about you when you're not in the room." Your business has to speak for itself.

To establish your brand and keep it cemented in people's minds, you need to:

1. Land on your name and logo
2. Develop a core message
3. Write, write, write
4. Be adaptable

Land on Your Name and Logo

First of all, you want to ensure that your brand name – which people take at face value – is easy to remember.

Sure, your friends and family may remember your business name easily if it's your name – but what about their networks? My friends and family obviously know how to spell "D'Alessio," but that relatability would deteriorate (fast) as my name moved beyond those closest to me. I'm not saying don't use your name for your business, if that's what you want to do, but if you have extra punctuation and more than two vowels like I do, you should consider an alternative.

The same goes for your logo and colors. Keep it simple. Know what you need your logo to do for you, and consider how that logo will look *wherever* it appears. Here are a few places you want to consider (some you are probably thinking of, and some you may not be):

- On a website (digital)
- On a business card (when printed, some colors don't exactly match the hue you may be looking for)
- Embroidered on a shirt (logos that are too intricate are difficult to embroider)
- Printed on promotional items (multiple colors will result in increased costs)
- On a small promotional item such as a pen or flash drive
- On your social media profiles (a circular version will often be needed to fit the space for your profile picture)

If your logo's too complicated or there are too many colors on it, you will struggle to get that level of detail printed on a small business card – and it will be even more of a struggle if you decide later to get your logo embroidered on a shirt or jacket. Furthermore, it's important to have both a vertical and horizontal logo, depending on where your logo will be placed. It would also be helpful to have a "secondary" logo that doesn't include your business name and is "shorter," which can be included on smaller items as well as in your social media profile photo. For me, that meant removing the name of my business altogether and simply using the book design at the left of my logo for social media profiles and other smaller destinations.

Landing on a logo and business name is no small feat, but it is only one part of the branding process. In Chapter 2, we discussed how important substance is for your business. You need to have a strong service offering beneath your name and logo. One way to ensure you are providing substance to your clients is to develop a strong and cohesive core message.

Develop a Core Message

One of the worst mistakes you can make in regard to your branding is to have conflicting messages. This usually occurs when a business has too many services that serve too many people. That's why knowing your ideal client and services (covered in Chapter 2) is helpful. Having this information will help you determine what your core message is and avoid the confusion that comes with having conflicting messages.

Your core message should be the reason why you do what you do. It's not *what* you do (that's your list of services), but it's *why* you do it. For example, "creating authentic stories and driving customers to action" is a core message of my business. This doesn't state what we do: social media management and content writing. It explains why we do it: so our clients' customers take action and purchase from them.

To develop your own core message, consider your "why." Why are you providing this service or product? What need does it solve? For me, my clients need more customers. They want their marketing to *do* something. Therefore, my services help create that action through storytelling. It's also important to tilt this message so it relates to your clients in a positive, beneficial way. For instance, perhaps you enjoy working with non-profits because it supports your giving and civic-minded spirit. That may be your "why," but it won't relate to your clients because it speaks to *your desire* versus *their need*. Ask yourself: Why do your services/products benefit your clients? What positive result will they have when they choose to work with you?

You will want to use your core message both implicitly and explicitly when discussing your business. It can be a part of your elevator pitch (more on that in Chapter 5), it can be part of your bio on your website, and it should be part of your social media marketing. You don't have to literally state your core message in every marketing piece or email you send out, but it should be the backbone of everything you do to drive business to your door. What I mean by this is you should use always drive people back to the *why* of working with you and the value you bring to them.

For example, when I decided that new business owners were *not* my ideal clients, I adjusted my core message, explicitly and implicitly:

Core Message	From:	To:
Implicit	We will collaborate in building your story together.	You, the client, are already established. You know who you are and you know what you do. Now, you just need a partner to help you get it out into the universe.
Explicit	Next Page will help you write the first pages of your business story!	You have a story. We'll help clients hear it.

This simple shift made it much easier for my core message to work for me. I didn't want to work with new business owners who didn't know who they were yet, so I simply adjusted my messaging to attract the right clients – ones who were more established.

Write, Write, Write

Remember that building brand awareness on social media takes time. You are unlikely to go viral in your first few months of business.

I was writing two to three blogs a month for nearly nine months before finally seeing a return on my time invested. You're going to need to be patient and consistent, just like I had to be. You'll also want to use the 80/20 Rule, which is a simple and effective way to ensure you are staying in front of your clients.

The 80/20 Rule

This is a content writing rule that is often used in sales presentations and proposals, but it works for marketing as well. Eighty per cent of your marketing (especially online, where you have virtually endless space to post) should inform, educate, or entertain. So, create personal posts. Share articles related to your industry. Post memes or graphics that are funny and related to your business (if that's on brand for you). The other twenty per cent of your marketing should be sales and self-promotional. By splitting your content into these two buckets, you'll not only increase the chances that you'll keep up with your marketing, but also keep your audience engaged, since you are providing informative, fun content that will keep them interested.

Be Adaptable

As you post more often and receive feedback, either in the form of engagement or verbal responses, you might realize that you need to adjust your brand to make it work better. This happened to me. The part of my brand I had to change was a very large part of my marketing strategy, which meant that I had to re-think how I was going to present my business to the world.

My business name and logo have served me well, and I am grateful for that. I've received numerous compliments on both, and they're inclusive enough that I've always had the wiggle room I needed to adapt my services. One part of my brand that did not work, however, was my tagline: *What's on your Next Page?* This may seem insignificant, but I was using it consistently as part of my brand. I used it as a hashtag, in emails, in proposals, on my website, and even on the customized sticky notes I'd designed to hand out at my first speaking engagement. The question was meant to evoke curiosity on the part of the reader. Did they know what was on their next page? Maybe they did, and they needed to hire someone for that next step. Maybe they didn't, and they needed to talk to someone about that. Either way, the hope was that they would think of me.

I decided to use this tagline as the basis for a six-month marketing campaign. I began reaching out to some friends and business partners I wanted to interview so I could share their answers on my social media channels. My question was: "*What's on your Next Page?*" Their answers were…well, let's just say, my campaign failed. Big time.

When I reached out to these women, there were nine originally on my list. Only four agreed to be featured. And I know – mainly because they told me – that the other five couldn't (or wouldn't) do it because of the question I had asked them.

I needed all of the posts to be similar in theme, right? And what was my ultimate question to all businesses and prospects and followers of my brand?

"What's on your Next Page?"

The vast majority of these women took pause when answering this question.

"I'm not really sure..."
"Well, it's kind of a long story..."
"I'm not sure I feel comfortable..."
"I'm kind of between two things right now..."

Most of these women were/are business owners, so I'd thought that the next page for business would be at least somewhat formed, but when I followed up with, "It can be about your personal life, not just work," that caused even more discomfort. This was actually a really good test for the authenticity of my brand. Authenticity is a major part of my core message. My business writes authentic stories, and yet, my hashtag "What's on your Next Page?" did not result in people providing authentic stories. If anything, it was a scary question that resulted in the paralysis of storytelling. When I became frustrated with the lack of responses, I took pause. Could I even ask myself that question?

After some thought, I realized that I did have a response, although I didn't know how comfortable I would be committing that to the eternal space of the Internet. At the time I had asked this question, my response could have changed based on the day. I might say, "On my Next Page, I am going to sign five more clients!" or "On my Next Page, I just want to keep the clients I have without feeling overwhelmed." Life is unpredictable, especially entrepreneurship.

What if that Next Page changed? What if the story line shifted? The characters changed? What if the whole damn book caught fire?

I couldn't keep authentically using that question as my tagline or in any of my marketing materials. I now understood the hesitation to answer it, and that the question itself created discomfort – not curiosity – in most people. So, I stopped asking the question: *"What's on your Next Page?"* and began stating: *"Let's turn the Next Page."* Marketing is about how people feel, and especially when you're a one-woman show, you've got to make every word work as hard as you do. When I shifted my tagline, people weren't put in an uncomfortable position anymore trying to figure out their answer and thinking, *Oh, crap, I have no idea,* leading them to an existential meltdown. They would now think: *There is a next page, and we're going to tackle it together.*

The need to adapt your branding might happen with your tagline, your business name, or your logo. It doesn't mean that your business has failed. You just need to pivot. After all, your business is essentially a living and breathing thing, so adjustments will be necessary as you learn more about your industry and your skill set.

Here are some signs that you might have to adjust your branding, along with some effective solutions:

Sign 1 Your Branding Isn't Working: The majority of your work involves you providing a small service you don't like doing.

Solution: Revisit your brand messaging. What are you saying and how are you saying it? What is the one service you don't want to do but are continually asked about? How can you remove any reference to that service?

Here is an example of how I overcame this hurdle. The problem? I often found that I was doing logo design, a service I don't particularly enjoy doing. This was because I wasn't specific enough with my brand messaging. In the early months of my business, I would say, "We provide branding services," which I thought would be effective. Unfortunately, people often think "brand" means logo design. And yes, logo design is *one part* of your brand, but not all of it. I was using too general a term, so clients assumed that meant logo design. To take this service off the menu, I shifted my service offering to state: "We provide brand messaging services: taglines, tone of voice and your business's origin story." "Messaging" clarified that our work was around words.

Sign 2 Your Branding Isn't Working: You're not closing business because prospective clients feel your prices are too expensive.

Solution: Examine whom you're marketing to and how you market to them. This is where a detailed "Ideal Client Map" helps. If you're speaking to a specific type of person, your language, your logo, and the "feel" of your marketing need to correlate to that person. This could be as specific as choosing to include a dollar sign with your prices. Does your ideal client shop where they like seeing "Only $9.99" on a price tag? Or does your ideal client enjoy meals at restaurants where *Market Price* next to an entrée makes the meal all the more enticing?

Sign 3 Your Branding Isn't Working: People are confused about what you offer.

Solution: Usually, potential clients are confused about what you offer because there's a problem with your business's logo and/or name. If going back to the drawing board to change your business logo and/or name is an absolute last resort for you, then you're going to need to adjust how you *speak* about your business.

I'll use my business as an example. With my logo being the image of a book and my business name being "Next Page Brand Strategies," my business could easily be mistaken for a marketing/branding service for authors. Yet, to date, I've had zero authors approach me about branding. That's because A) I've been strategic in whom I speak to about my services and B) I always mention specific services that I know will resonate with business owners: social media marketing, content writing, blogging, and so on. Using the right vocabulary – consistently – has framed what people should expect from my business.

HOW TO REACH YOUR IDEAL CLIENT

By year three of running my business, I was beginning to realize who my ideal client was: a man in his fifties or sixties who was ready to pass on his business to someone younger, and who wanted to get his marketing "up to date." He needed (or wanted) to get *his* name and face out of networking and capitalize on his already-established brand. This is how LinkedIn became my number one online referral source.

There are three very specific reasons why LinkedIn was the right channel to generate online business for me. On LinkedIn, I could find the people who were 1) in the age range I was targeting, 2) interested in the service I was providing, and 3) educated about my service on such a level that they would feel I was the right person (well, business) for the job.

When you're figuring out where to find your ideal client online so you can reach them, you have to think about these reasons. It helps to put them in the form of a question. Below, I've demonstrated how, by asking these questions, I was able to determine where I would be able to find, and then reach out to, my clients online. When you examine your online options, ask yourself these three questions:

Reason 1: What is the age range I am targeting?
The majority of active users on this platform (LinkedIn) were the age range I was targeting (fifty to sixty).

Reason 2: Am I providing a service or product? Is it B2B or B2C?
People are more open to professional service marketing on a B2B platform, such as LinkedIn. Facebook, which favors B2C marketing, was not the right fit for me.

> **Reason 3: How educated (on the industry/ service/product) does my client need to be?**
> *The final reason LinkedIn worked for me is because I was targeting clients who already knew the value of marketing and what it would do for their business.*

To make sure you reach your ideal client online, you'll need to do the following:

1. Review your "client avatar" in Chapter 2.
2. Determine the best online channels on which to reach your ideal clients. Here's a quick rundown of where you should begin:
   a. Facebook: Active audiences are moms with young children and grandparents
   b. Twitter: Active audiences are men, sports-specific industries, and non-profits
   c. LinkedIn: Active audiences are people aged thirty-five to fifty-five and retired Baby Boomers
   d. Pinterest: Active audiences are stay-at-home moms
   e. Instagram: Active audiences are women aged twenty to thirty-five who have an interest in food, drink, makeup and photography
   f. Snapchat: Active audiences are high-school students aged fifteen to eighteen and their parents
3. Download a scheduling platform. For example, Hootsuite or Sprout Social.

4. Create a Content Calendar. HubSpot and Hootsuite have free online resources to help you do this.
5. Consider other content you may want to use for social media:
   a. Blogs
   b. Videos
   c. An e-newsletter
   d. Audio files from podcasts
6. Start tracking how people hear about you

In your first year in business, when people ask how you've gotten clients, you'll most likely say, "Word of mouth." This is the most common form of marketing for all new business owners (and seasoned business owners, to be honest). What's important to remember is that "word of mouth" is more than one person telling another person about your service. That might be the final push they need to contact you, but I can almost guarantee that, if you're creating enough of the right digital content, you'll receive that connection and introduction on the heels of an e-newsletter you sent out or a Facebook post you scheduled. Think strategically about what type of content is "shareable," because you never know where it might end up.

WRITE THE RIGHT CONTENT

During my first year in business, photos of my dog, Max, received a higher engagement rate than any other photo I posted on social media. He was the perfect model. I remember how, when I had a new webinar to promote, it was so easy to include him in my marketing for the event. All I had to do was get out my laptop, stick the dog in front of the screen, place his paws on the keyboard, and snap a photo. Max is a hound mix, so he has the wrinkled characteristics of a basset hound, and that, combined with the fact that he really doesn't enjoy when I try posing him for pictures, was perfect for my post. My caption read: "Feeling down about your social media strategy? We can help." People connected. People responded. My brand started to grow beyond the feeds of my friends and family. They came for the dog. They stayed for the marketing.

On average, my social media posts at the time had an engagement rate of about ten per cent. That means about ten per cent of my followers would like, comment or share my posts. Whenever a post included a photo of Max, however, the engagement rate would go up to between twenty to thirty per cent, even if the content itself had nothing to do with marketing.

This just goes to show that the content you share can make a big difference to the success of your business. Here are some ways to approach content for your business:

1. Create content that comes naturally to you
2. Be engaging with your content

Create Content Naturally

During my first year of business, I was consistently blogging – for two very important reasons:

1. It added SEO to my website

2. It gave me an outlet to connect with people in a way that was enjoyable for me

For you, creating content that comes naturally to you may mean creating educational videos or sharing photography. Consider where you are most comfortable when interacting with others and how you can use that to your advantage. Here are a few ideas:

1. Are you comfortable speaking with people in person? Consider virtual or in-person webinars that are interactive.
2. Are you comfortable taking photos? Consider focusing on your Instagram channel to market your business – even if your business isn't a photography business! Take photos that represent what you do.
3. Are you comfortable writing? Consider writing blogs or an e-newsletter and pushing that content out to your social media followers.

Do What Comes Naturally to You with Your Content

When I meet with people who are struggling to write content, I am often reminded of my days as a teacher. Unless a student loved to write, they would freeze at the sight of a blank page. They felt as though everything needed to come out perfectly, and that every word needed to have significant meaning. If this is how you feel, keep in mind that, when it comes to the content you create for your business, most people are not reading/analyzing every word that you choose. As long as your overall strategy is focused around your core message, you are saying exactly what you need to say.

What really matters is that you do what comes naturally to you already. How do you do this? Simply create and use content that you would normally use in your online habits. Your pets. Your family. You taking a selfie in the morning because you are rocking that new blazer. Do it. It's all usable content to keep you in front of your audience. When you use content like this, not only does it frame your business as approachable and "personable," but it also helps you to gain confidence in this new arena of "marketing yourself," because you're working in an environment that you're already comfortable in.

Be Engaging with Your Content

By now, I've shared that Max was the perfect model for my business. In fact, he was in more of my business's social media posts than I was, and I was completely content with that.

Well, one time, I thought it might be a good idea to post something without a picture of him in it. A friend suggested I post more about marketing tips and "how to build your brand" on social media – it's something they wanted to see more of. So, I diligently scheduled the next month's posts to be centered around that: one new marketing tip every week. I even created a video and boosted it to my followers and their friends to encourage them to like our social media pages so that they wouldn't miss out on my tips.

By week three of this experiment, one thing was very clear: This was not what the vast majority of my followers wanted to see. Engagement was down by fifty per cent (*fifty per cent!*) compared to my other posts that usually included the Charlotte skyline or a photo of Max being a dog.

What did I do? Well, the following month, I went back to posting photos of Max at various spots in Charlotte (we focused on breweries – because nothing says Charlotte more than dogs at breweries). It may not have had anything to do with marketing suggestions for small businesses – but hey, if the people wanted more photos of my dog lying around, I wasn't going to complain. (P.S. Engagement picked right back up [by fifty per cent] once I began sharing photos of Max again.)

What did I learn from this?

Your content may not be what you think it should be. Yes, you should explain your business, who you are, and other important facts that will encourage people to work with you. However, you also need to hook them. Engage them. If you're running a young business in its first year that doesn't have a strong reputation yet, consider these five ways to grab people's attention.

How to Create Engaging Content

Here are a few ways to engage your audience on social media and inspire them to take action. Their actions will either implicitly (in the form of brand awareness) or explicitly (in the form of sales) support your brand.

1. Ask questions: This will help you learn information about your audience as well as invite them to be a part of the conversation.

2. Invite expression: Consider how you "brand" your social media. Is it a hashtag? Is it asking your audience to post a silly selfie and tag your business?[8]

3. Provide an offer: Consider how you can have special "deals" or packages for particular audiences during certain times of the year. Can you market to Veterans around Veteran's Day in November? How about moms in May?

4. Get personal: No, your audience does not need to know everything about your personal life. What are some safe topics you feel you can share? Pets are always safe. What about the history of the name of your business? While you're building a brand, invite opportunities where your audience can connect with you as a human being.

5. Partner: I am always an advocate of businesses supporting each other. I always recommend to my clients that if we promote a partner of theirs, this partner should promote them as well. Cross-posting and sharing content is an easy and supportive way to reach new audiences in a mutually beneficial relationship.

---

[8] Feldman, Barry. "5 Proven Social Media Engagement Strategies for 2020." *HubSpot Blog*, 2020, blog.hubspot.com/marketing/proven-social-media-engagement-strategies.

BUILD A CONNECTION

In addition to creating an online presence for your business and branding it for your ideal client, you'll need to reach out and connect with your ideal clients one on one. To do this effectively, you'll want to:

1. Learn about sales
2. Be consistent and likeable
3. Be clear (and assertive) about payment
4. Move on from rejection

Learn About Sales

In year one of my business, sales were the last thing I wanted to do. This was counterintuitive, since doing sales should have been one of the first five things on my to-do list when starting out. Now, years later, it's one of my favorite aspects of running a business. Why? Because I enjoy getting to know people. Also, I've learned that doing sales looks very different to what I'd originally expected it to look like. Before I owned my business, I hadn't thought I was the kind of person who would be good at doing sales. This is what I thought a successful salesperson would look like:

Successful Salesperson
- Extremely extroverted
- Loud
- Humorous
- Charming

- A sleek dresser with perfectly styled hair and perfect makeup (image is everything, right?)
- Always smiling

This was how I saw myself:

- Introverted
- Usually getting talked over on conference calls
- Often telling killer grammar jokes
- Sarcastic
- Dealing with my curly hair often being one temperature point away from becoming a frizz ball
- Often having a serious demeanor (usually because I'm deep in thought)

You'd think, from looking at my personality traits, that I wouldn't be successful when it comes to sales, or, at least, that's what I thought. The thing is, though, that potential clients have a lot of options when it comes to whom they choose to do business with, whatever the industry. It's not just about being the perfect salesperson – it's about being the right fit. That's why I was able to find success, even if I didn't think I would when it came to sales. In your case, whether or not you have the "stereotypical salesperson" traits above, clients will have a variety of reasons for why they want to work with you. They might want to work with you because they like you or because they find you clever and funny or because there was that one time you helped them with a small project and they thought, *I need to remember to call her again.*

For me, I found that my quiet personality worked in my favor during the sales process. If I sent an email, it was quick and to the point, usually sharing an article or upcoming event that I thought might be valuable to my contact. When they responded with a question or comment, I would respond thoughtfully and ask another question. I wasn't going to waste their time with a lot of talk. For clients who respected that and wanted someone to cut through the noise, this became a selling point.

The fact is, being successful at sales isn't about being the right kind of person. It's about understanding how the sales process works. Now, I wish I could give you strategies on honing your perfect sales persona, but that's best suited for a sales or business coach. Instead, what I *will* give you is one important piece of advice that works for everyone: You won't know what sales style works for you until you're "out in the field." Preparing to go into sales is similar to reading about how to swim or practicing the breaststroke while sitting on the couch in your living room. Until you're physically in the water, doing the activity, you won't know what it will feel like or what will be most comfortable for you. So, it's only once you're doing sales that you'll learn what your sales style is.

First important task: You've got to get out there. If you don't start a conversation, you'll never make a sale. And if you're an introvert like me, I'm with you on the pain of this. However, I was able to get over this by realizing the first sentence out of my mouth didn't need to be (and shouldn't have been) a sales pitch. Instead, I simply needed to ask someone their name and what they did for a living. Many people have said to me, "You're an introvert?" They squint at me skeptically, then say, "Really?" But I am. I like to be left alone most of the time, and when there are dozens of people at an event, whether in person or online (and even if I know them), I feel fairly anxious.

I know the stigma. Introvert can be a dirty word sometimes. If you connect with this sentiment, I encourage you to read the book *Quiet: The Power of Introverts in a World That Can't Stop Talking* by Susan Cain. But whether you're an extrovert, an introvert, or an ambivert, I just want to assure you that your personality type does not dictate how successful you will be at owning a business or making sales. There are some very extroverted people I know who struggle to keep their business afloat, and there are very quiet introverts I know who are doing very well. It's not about your general personality type. It's about being a living, breathing human being.

Your Innate Personality

However, putting yourself out there and practicing doing sales when you *also* have a good understanding of what your personality type is will definitely work in your favor. That's because you'll be able to recognize the common traits you bring to any interaction/relationship in your life, including with potential clients. Whether you are more extroverted in your communication style or you are more often known as "the fixer," your personality style will inherently shape how you sell.

To understand sales, you'll want to take a personality test (even if you have before) that gives you detailed results that pinpoint where your strengths and weaknesses are. Many business coaches offer this type of test and are certified in providing an assessment of how to best read the results. You can also find free tests online, although paid tests typically provide more detailed results. Keep in mind that the Myers-Briggs personality assessment is considered outdated at this point, even if it's the one most of us are familiar with. There are several others that many executive coaches and leaders use when assessing their teams. Here are some of the big ones:

DISC: This assessment categorizes personalities into four buckets – Dominance, Influence, Steadiness, and Conscientiousness – and measures your tendencies and preferences, or patterns or behavior, within each.

Big 5: As its name suggests, this assessment will examine your personality dimensions in five areas – Openness, Conscientiousness, Agreeableness, Extraversion, and Neuroticism.

Strengths Finder: Often used when people are considering a professional change, this assessment focuses on revealing your innate strengths and how to then apply them to your career.

Enneagram: This assessment categorizes people into nine personality types and demonstrates how each personality interacts with the world around them.

After you have taken one (or more!) of these assessments, consider which parts can be used in your sales process. For example, is spontaneity a part of your personality? This can translate into seeming fun-loving and versatile for some clients, while it may seem scattered and unorganized to others. How can you use this

GET YOUR BUSINESS OUT THERE

trait to your advantage and in what ways can you adapt to reach the clients this trait doesn't speak to? Some parts of your personality may work really well, while others create hurdles between you and potential clients. For instance, I am a cerebral person and prefer to have time to think through a question before I answer. However, this doesn't work when I'm in the middle of presenting a proposal to a potential client who asks a lot of questions. No one is going to give me ten minutes to find the exact answer, therefore, I needed to practice how to give a *non-answer* if I truly don't know and re-direct the conversation back to the topic at hand.

The truth is, regardless of your personality type, this will take practice in front of actual clients. The good news is, the more people you meet and talk with, the better at this process you'll become.

Be Consistent and Likeable

My dad once told me a story from when he was in outside sales in the trucking industry back in the '80s. He called on a prospective client every month for years, just to check in. He never got a face-to-face with the gentleman. What my dad was selling, this guy didn't need. But he was my dad's White Whale – that ideal Big Client. So even as the years went by, my dad continued to chase him.

After three years had passed, my dad was in his office one day when the phone rang. "Well, Jimmie," said the voice on the end of the line, "today is your lucky day." It was his prospect who finally needed his services, and my dad was the first person on his list of people to

119

call. It was the largest account my dad had landed by that point in his career, and, in fact, he stayed friends with that gentleman for decades, even after my dad moved on to another company and they were no longer working together.

My dad got that sale because he had been consistent. He never stopped making those phone calls (email didn't exist then), no matter how much of a "waste of time" they seemed to be. And he had always been friendly and courteous when leaving messages, even though he could have easily been like, "Seriously? Can't you just call me back? I call you every month!"

Here's the lesson of this story: To be successful in sales, you need to be 1) consistent, and 2) likeable. Sure, there are a lot of sales books out there – and I've read most of them – but, whatever you might learn from them, the most important thing to know is that being successful in sales is really as simple as doing these two things. Be consistent. Be likeable.

Be Consistent

Being consistent is about being there when you say you will. If you're going to call someone, call them. If you're going to reach back out in two weeks at a specific time, do it. People have short attention spans. And no matter how awesome you are, they're going to forget about you unless you stay in front of them. If you're not staying in front of them, others will outsell you.

To help you with being consistent, I recommend implementing a sales pipeline system as soon as you can. Whether you're using a robust CRM (Customer Relationship Management) system, like SalesForce or HubSpot, or you're simply opening a spreadsheet, figure out how to keep track of whom you're calling, what the details of that call are, and set a reminder for when you will reach out next.

For a long time, I simply had a large whiteboard in my office with a list of names I was actively chasing written on it. I would change the color of the ink I used to write their name in anytime I reached a new level in the sales process with them (phone call, meeting, open proposal), and I would write a "next reach-out date" to the left of their name. Then, I would set a reminder on my calendar and start the process all over again with the next name. After a couple of years, I really needed a better system, in large part because my whiteboard couldn't hold all the leads I was chasing. Eventually, when I could afford it, I moved to an online system.

Once you begin your sales process, consider where you may be lacking in keeping everything organized. If a spreadsheet, whiteboard, or other free resource isn't working for you, there are a lot of great CRM systems for small businesses. Online platforms can range in cost from $250 to $3,000 a year. If those numbers scare you, don't worry. Many high-quality CRM systems, such as Monday or Asana, cost closer to $250 to $500 a year. At the end of the day, like everything in business, it's all about figuring out what works best for you.

Be Likeable

I was always pretty good at staying consistent. But when it came to the second of these two rules – be likeable – that was a little tougher for me. Mainly because, as I've mentioned, I'm an introvert.

Don't get me wrong, I'm friendly, but it does take a while for me to get to a jovial place with people. So, I had to learn how to do this more quickly and in a way that still felt authentic to me. Because, when it comes to sales, nothing will sink you quicker than phoniness.

In order to be likeable and build connections, I began relying on parts of my personality that had nothing to do with marketing. That way, I could build my likeability, which would then build trust, and which would, then, in turn, build my client list. Here is a list of things that I began to use in my sales and marketing strategy that built likeability:

1. My dog, Max
2. Yoga and meditation
3. Traveling
4. My dog, Max
5. Me not being a morning person
6. Books and literature
7. My relationship with my family
8. My former career as a teacher

When you consider how to connect with people, by creating a list like this and knowing what topics to bring up with whom, it may come very naturally to you. You'll notice I have my dog listed more than once on this list. That's because he comes up a lot. Talking about my dog is an easy way for me to connect with many people in my network. But (believe it or not) Max doesn't appeal to everyone. If I'm talking to a potential client who has three kids running around, talking about Max probably isn't the best choice. That's when I can talk instead about my relationship with my family or about my previous job as a teacher. When you put together your own list of potential topics to talk about, be aware of your clients' interests, too.

Although I've mentioned that being an introvert can be a hurdle for connecting with people, I would also caution extroverts on how they approach people. No matter your personality type, if you're trying to connect with someone who flat out does not understand or care about the topic you're discussing, then you're not connecting. Sounds simple, right? Well, it isn't to a lot of people. Unfortunately, I've witnessed too many people who have an agenda in mind for a conversation who cannot adapt to what is happening in front of them. This happens all the time in the business world.

Adapting is hugely important, not just in business, but in any conversation where you want to hold your audience's attention. I learned this when I was a teacher. I had to adapt to the audience in front of me, and sometimes that meant throwing out the lesson I had planned.

If you come into a business conversation hoping to speak to someone about your shared connection of having a spouse/children of the same age/dogs/the same alma mater or working in the same industry – you may not actually be able to connect. This attempt has the potential to backfire. Some people are very private about their personal lives, and others may have had a negative experience at your shared school or within your shared industry. I often start with a simple connection (about my dog) because it feels safe, but then, if there isn't a connection, I switch to another topic. Weather's always a good one. That may sound shallow, but weather is a small-talk subject for a reason: It starts you in a safe place.

Here in the South, especially in summer, I'm often commenting about the heat. If I talk about the heat and the other person doesn't notice it, then I'll talk about my propensity for the cold because I was born in the Northeast. This often leads to my story of when I slept in an ice hotel (the only one in North America) in Quebec, Canada for my thirtieth birthday. This story usually sets me apart from other "marketers," and clients love to talk about it. Just like that, weather leads to a connection.

Be Clear (and Assertive) About Payment

Since we're talking about reaching out to clients about your services, you may be wondering, *Okay, that all sounds good, but how do I get paid?* You may not be wondering (but you should be), *What happens if someone doesn't pay me?*

Conversations with clients about payment are tough for a lot of new business owners. And it can often be tougher for women – at least, that's what I've heard. Perhaps men just assert their confidence in their value a little more easily than women. So, ladies, assert your confidence in what you are worth. In other words, don't be me when I first started out, undervaluing myself for the first six months of my business. Instead, be me now. Now, I am assertive. I confidently say to clients, "My hourly rate is X." The best news of all? The over-whelming majority of my clients never pause on my hourly rate. I say it's X and they reply, "Sounds good." Be confident. Know your worth.

Now, when it comes to the process of getting that money into your bank account, you'll end up splitting client payments into several categories. Why? Clients are more than likely going to do what is easiest for them, but not necessarily what's best for you. As your business grows, you can outline your preferred way of getting paid. But in the beginning, you'll likely have to be more flexible. Here are a few ways you can get paid, and the pros and cons of each:

Type of Payment	Pros	Cons
Credit Card	Easy for your client, therefore, a quicker payment.	You'll have to pay a processing fee or pass that fee onto your client.
Check	You get all the money.	Can take weeks or months if your client isn't organized or is facing a cash shortage.
Venmo	Easy for your client.	Money doesn't arrive automatically to your account. You'll need to log in to ensure the money is transferred. This delays you getting the cash.
ACH Direct Deposit	You get all the money and get it quickly.	More complicated setup for your client, so they're less likely to agree to paying this way.

During your first year of business, I recommend the easiest option, which is accepting credit cards. It's unlikely you are making very large transactions where the processing fee will eat into a large part of your income. Today, the majority of my clients still pay by credit card. Although the processing fees probably add up to several hundred dollars for the year, for me, it's worth the convenience (read: happiness) for my clients and the security in knowing I'm going to have that cash in my bank account not long after I send an invoice, versus waiting a month (or more) for a check to arrive in the mail.

When it comes to getting paid in your first year of business, you'll want to do the following whenever you can:

- ✓ Ask for payment up front (or at least part of it). This is common. It shouldn't seem weird to your client. If they feel uncomfortable about it, ask why.

- ✓ Outline a clear payment process for your client on how you like to be paid (see above).

- ✓ Establish *net terms*, or, in other words, the amount of days that a client needs to pay you in from the day they are invoiced. I began with thirty days, but quickly realized that I needed to change that number, because I was working for a full month before ever seeing a dime, and my bank account couldn't handle that. Now, I'm at ten-day terms, and most of my clients are on board with that. Some of my larger clients with whom I have a long-term relationship have stayed on thirty-day terms because A) they are writing bigger checks and B) I know they'll pay me because of our history.

✓ Create a late payment fee if it takes longer than thirty days for a client to pay you, and have it in writing (either in your contract, your invoice, or both). I learned this lesson too late. A late payment fee (usually five per cent) encourages clients to pay on time so you're not chasing money later. And if you do end up chasing the money, then at least you'll make more money when you finally get paid.

Sometimes, you won't be able to control these scenarios, and you'll have to take what you can get. I know; I've been there. But when you can, follow the advice above, as it's best practice.

Move on from Rejection

Let's say you've done all the "right" things. You've practiced "talking sales" with potential clients, you've been out making contacts, and you've connected with people by being consistent and likeable. But you keep getting rejected. That's normal – more often than not, especially when you first begin your business, you're going to be hearing, "No thanks."

If someone doesn't want to do business with you, it'll feel a little like a romantic rejection. Putting your heart out there and feeling like you're both on the same page and that there's a real connection, and then suddenly – bam! They slam the door of opportunity. "This isn't a good fit," they say, or they stop following up on your calls and emails until finally responding with, "We're no longer interested." Was it something you said? Did you accidentally offend them at one time? It's a rejection, plain and simple. And rejection hurts. But it doesn't lower your value, and it doesn't mean you're not awesome. You just need to find the right person who recognizes your awesomeness. In the meantime, you'll need to deal with rejection so that it doesn't bring you down or get in the way of running your business successfully.

Here are some strategies for dealing with rejection:

1. Vent. Don't pretend it doesn't bother you (unless it really, truly doesn't). Talk to your support network about how much it sucks to get rejected and about how frustrated you are.

2. Step away. Especially if it's a big rejection, you're going to need to step away from your business for a moment. Take a drive. Go for a walk. Do something that gets you far away from your desk.

3. Act. Now, when you're feeling rejected, is a great time for you to ask for some love from the clients that you're currently working with. Ask them to provide a testimonial or write a review on Google, Facebook, or LinkedIn. This will also check the box for marketing content that you can use in the future.

End-of-Chapter Check-In

EXERCISE 1: BRANDING 101
BRAND YOUR BUSINESS

It's important to know *why* you have your business. Try this exercise to develop your core message:

I created my business to solve _____ (problem) for my clients.

Solving problems for my clients makes me feel _____ (emotion).

Solving this problem makes my clients feel _____ (emotion).

Use at least two of the above words/phrases you wrote above to create a core message. (Example: We provide **stress-free** accounting services so **owners can focus** on running their business.)

EXERCISE 2: REACH YOUR IDEAL CLIENT ONLINE
MARKET YOUR BUSINESS

When marketing your business to your ideal client online, you need to know specific details for your strategy to be effective. Answer these questions so you can begin building the foundation of your marketing strategy:

1. Who is your ideal client?

2. Which of these channels does your client interact with on a daily basis? (Circle all that apply, but circle no more than three to keep your marketing manageable):

   Facebook   Instagram   Twitter   Snapchat

   Pinterest   LinkedIn   Other: _____

3. What days and times are you going to post? Repeat this every week for at least three months before trying out a different schedule.

4. Set up a spreadsheet (or other document) and begin tracking: How Did You Hear About Us? Ask this question in your first email with a potential client or on your first phone call. Make it a natural part of your questioning for your sales process.

EXERCISE 3: WRITE THE RIGHT CONTENT

What is your 80/20 breakdown? Here's how to figure it out:

1. Eighty per cent of your content needs to be informative, educational, or personal. What are two reputable sources in your industry you can use for content? Bookmark these two sources and check their website/blog/social media channels at least once a month for content that you can re-share.

2. Twenty per cent of your content needs to be promotional. What services or deals do you want to promote? (For example, in the case of deals: "Purchase one of our headshot photography packages this month and we'll throw in an extra re-touched photo.")

EXERCISE 4: BUILD A CONNECTION

What are the things that make *you* you? What do you do when you're not hustling? What defines you in a way that makes you human? Nobody cares that I can create and target Facebook ads with high click-through rates. A lot of people can do that. What makes them sign on the dotted line is *me*.

Who are you? What's your story? Here are some creative prompts to get you thinking outside the box.

1. What is your favorite guilty-pleasure TV show?

   _____

2. What is your most-used emoji?

   _____

3. If you could bring back any fashion trend, what would it be?

   _____

4. What's an illogical fear you have?

   _____

5. What's your go-to karaoke song?

   _____

5

Get Yourself Out There

A h, the elevator pitch. If you haven't come across this yet in business (and you will), this is what an elevator pitch refers to: You are in a theoretical elevator with your ideal client and they ask you what you do. You have the length of that elevator ride (thirty seconds) to explain it to them –and pique their interest in working with you.

Elevator pitches are really, really hard for me because, although I'm shy at first, I'm also Italian American, which means that, when I *do* start talking, I have a lot to say. Simply talking about "where I grew up" requires listing four states, explaining three moves during my childhood, and the inevitable follow-up conversation that, no, my dad was not in the military.

That's a problem, because mastering your elevator pitch is a big deal. Knowing how to sum up your business in only thirty seconds can be really useful, especially when you're talking to potential high-paying clients. But it's also unnerving. Talking to people about your business and knowing that whatever you say – or don't say – could be the difference between paying your mortgage that month or pulling from your savings (again) is terrifying. This can make anyone, even an extrovert, tongue-tied.

So, I had to improve my elevator pitch, even if I was struggling with it. To do this, I decided to hit the timer on my phone and see what I could get out without feeling rushed. It took some practice, but I got it down to fifty-three seconds. After a few more tries, I was down to fifty-one seconds and then disastrously up to one minute and six seconds. After struggling a bit more, and getting down to forty-nine seconds, I decided my elevator ride was taking us to the top of the Empire State Building and that my passengers were just going to have to be cool with that.

The truth is, as long as what you are saying is informative to the listener, it's okay to go over thirty seconds. Now, there will be some networking events where they physically time you to keep it to thirty seconds (or less), and in that case, you may need to improvise and ensure your most important information is at the front-end of your pitch, but for the most part, clocking in at forty-nine seconds, or even a minute and ten seconds, is likely not going to make or break your relationship with that person.

Think of your elevator pitch as a teaser, or trailer, for the movie that is your business. The important thing is to speak confidently, clearly, and to provide the important highlights of your service or product so that people want to learn more about what you do.

This is what I had it boiled down to:

1. Who I am: Cassandra
2. What I do: Social media marketing
3. Whom I do it for: Small businesses
4. Why I do it (this is likely a version of your core message): I help small businesses share authentic stories that drive customers to action

People connected with my elevator pitch for two reasons: 1) I was usually speaking to someone who was a small business owner or someone who knew a small business owner and 2) I had a hook. I said why I did something without explaining how I did it. Now, they were curious, and they might ask me: "How does storytelling translate to clients taking action?" "What services do you provide that make this possible?" In my elevator pitch, I was giving just enough information so that the right client, or someone who knew the right client, would begin to ask more questions.

By creating my elevator pitch and sharing it with people, I was getting myself out there as a business leader. Getting yourself out there is a very important element of running a successful business, whether you're meeting people in person, over a virtual networking event, or through a Facebook group. Often, that means understanding your personality type and using it to enhance your strengths.

Other times, it means being authentic when you're in front of people.

> **In this chapter, you'll learn how to get yourself out there most effectively. To do this, you need to:**
> 1. Find out who you are
> 2. Understand the link between your business and your reputation
> 3. Beat imposter syndrome with sincerity

FIND OUT WHO YOU ARE

As I've mentioned, I'm an introvert. This means that, unlike extroverts, I get my energy from being alone. So, while an extrovert can go from a morning of back-to-back meetings to lunch with a client, and then give an afternoon presentation and still have energy by the end of the day, I need to be more careful with my scheduling.

When I started my business, and I began scheduling out my days and appointments, I learned (pretty quickly) that three was the magic number. That was how many meetings (virtual, in person, or on the phone) I could do in a day successfully. If I had a fourth meeting scheduled, I would be tapped out by then. So, I began scheduling my days with this important piece of information in mind. I made sure if I had three calls scheduled in the morning that my afternoon would be spent working quietly on my laptop. Vice versa, if I had a late meeting or event scheduled, I made sure that I hadn't stacked too many meetings throughout the day so that I'd have enough energy left for that late meeting or event.

That's another key lesson here. You need to know what gives you energy and what drains it, and some of it may be trial and error in the beginning if you're unsure. Learning this will help you be at your best when running your business. Build your schedule to it. Know what will make *you* most successful (not what other people tell you that is). If something won't mesh with your schedule, be the boss, and choose not to do it. You can make that call.

By finding out who you are, you can learn what schedule gives you the most energy, what strategies make you most productive, and more. To do this, you need to do two things:

1. Know your personality beyond a test
2. Be your best self

Know Your Personality Beyond a Test

In the last chapter, I explained the importance of personality tests and how they can help you understand your own sales process. However, there are some things that a personality test will likely not tell you and of which you need to be aware. I've mentioned that I'm Italian American. Sicilian, to be specific. There isn't a personality test that identifies or explains what that means. However, I know that, for me, it means I have a short temper. I get angry and frustrated when people aren't pulling their weight or are complaining without making adjustments to their situation. When I'm in a conversation that escalates, I find myself at the point beyond anger where I just stop talking (which isn't productive).

Since I know this about myself, I do my best to manage it. If I receive an email and start to feel my blood boil, I take a breath, get up from my desk, and take the dog for a quick walk before I sit down to write a response. And even then, sometimes my response isn't send-worthy, so I need to wait one more day. There are several business owners I've worked with who've commented on how "chill" I seem, or how I always have a positive attitude about a difficult project. "It's practice," I say, because it is, and because I'm taking care of myself outside of those conversations.

You have to know your personality and address how it works and doesn't work for your business in the same way. To do this, take a look at your relationships outside of your business. How you relate to people and difficult situations is usually similar across the board. Think more specifically about your romantic relationship or another close relationship, like one you have with a sibling or best friend. What has triggered you in the past or caused you to either lose your temper or feel very overwhelmed and stressed? How did you handle it? More importantly, how do you wish you handled it? Think of how you might handle it in a similar way when going through the same emotion in the context of your business.

Be Your Best Self

I left one of my corporate jobs not long after I had been reproached for my gaps. As discussed in Chapter 2, a gap is often described in business as an area in which you aren't meeting an expected deliverable.

Gaps can often be related to your personality type. For example, of The Big 5 personality traits, in conscientiousness I rank closer to "careful" versus "impulsive." As stated before, personality traits are simply ways in which you process and live within the world around you; there is no one trait that is better or worse than another. This is important to keep in mind.

In my previous corporate job, I was asked to overcome this specific gap of being too "careful." Since I was in charge of the company's Facebook page, I was very conscientious about what went out under the business's name. Especially when a topic was political or sensitive, I wanted to pause and reflect on how this might be received by our audience and whom we might alienate if we posted such content. However, my supervisor believed part of our company's mission was to share this important content regardless of how it was received by our followers. My careful approach of viewing the content from all angles did not fit the job they wanted me to do. Could I have posted that content without thinking of the consequences? I could (and I did), but it made me extremely uncomfortable both as a person and, more importantly, as a marketer. I was going against my gut instincts.

The lesson to take away from this is that when you know more about your habits and personality traits, you can best position yourself for how to be successful with your clients. You will probably be questioned about a certain way you handle business, like I was with my former supervisor. Knowing *why* you are that way and being able to articulate *how* that's good for business will set you apart. Remember: Your traits are not a "gap" to overcome; they are simply a part of who you are and it's important for you to find the right people who can connect with you in that same way. I was not a good fit for my old job because they wanted someone who took risks. However, now I work with businesses where carefulness is highly valued and appreciated. My conscientiousness is a selling point.

But just because you know your habits and traits, it doesn't mean that you are always right, right? Always be mindful of where you do need to improve and recognize these areas as growth opportunities. Here are some examples:

1. More technology training on a specific program or software
2. Better organization or support if goals aren't being met
3. Better understanding of an internal process that you currently don't understand (for example, how to get budgets approved)
4. Learning how to manage job-related tasks you struggle with

Here are a few examples of areas that should never be considered gaps, and which you should not be expected to change:

1. Your personality
2. Whether you are an introvert or extrovert
3. Your boundaries

4. How you manage stress (as long as it's healthy for you and others)

Strategies for Being Your Best Self

Knowing yourself well is one of the most important elements of being a successful entrepreneur. When you know yourself well, you're able to focus your energy on the areas you need to grow in your business and shut out the noise of anyone or anything else not helping you. When you've done the research and have insight into your own personality, you should have a good idea of where you need to move the needle. It's all about knowing yourself so you can be your best self.

Ask yourself these questions to get started with developing your best-self strategies:

1. How do you best communicate? Phone? Email? In person?
2. How do you usually manage stress? Be honest. How can you incorporate this into your schedule as a proactive instead of reactive solution?
3. Who is a trusted confidante when you need an honest opinion on how to handle a difficult situation?

Write the answers to these questions on a piece of paper and place it near your desk. Keep these tips in mind when A) communicating with clients in an effective way, B) managing stress at the end of a long day or week, and C) looking for support from someone you trust. It's important to have these tools always ready since we can't always predict when we might need them.

You will continuously receive feedback (whether implicit or explicit) from others throughout your entrepreneurial journey. Determine what information is constructive when it comes to helping you serve your clients better, and have someone you trust around who can give you reliable feedback on how to manage any gaps that may be keeping you from becoming your best self.

YOUR BUSINESS, YOUR REPUTATION

In the early days of running your business, most people will be unable to extricate you from your business and vice versa. You might even choose to add elements of your personality to your business. I knew that when I started a business with a reference to literature in the name and logo that most of my friends and family would appreciate the nod to my personality: a book nerd.

When I got a tattoo a few years later, I realized that I was even more intertwined with my business than I'd thought. Before getting my first tattoo, I'd researched a lot of book images without thinking much about my business logo, since, in my head, that was obviously a separate thing. However, when friends saw my new tattoo, more than one replied, "Oh, cool! Is that your logo?"

Oh, no.

It wasn't, and it hadn't even occurred to me that people might assume that was a possibility. A friend at the time put it into perspective for me: "Hey," he said, "there are only so many ways you can draw an open book." He had a point.

The important thing to keep in mind – whether or not you're planning to get a tattoo that's vaguely similar to your business logo – is that you need to remember that people are going to see you as the business and the business as you. Especially when you're starting out, *you* are your brand. It's not about having a cool logo or a fancy website. If you're running your business right, people see beyond all that branding and see who you – and your business – actually are.

Your business brand is an extension of you. I'm a marketing professional, so naturally I want to tell you all the ways that you can best market your business, but there is something you should know: In your first year of business, people are not going to do business with you because of your marketing. Here, your marketing will work as a way to stay in front of people. *Pound the streets. Shake hands and kiss babies. Hustle.* Whatever you want to call it, but it all means the same thing: Stay in front of people even if you think it's not working. You will have heard this before if you have done any networking, but I'll repeat for those who have not: People need to *know, like* and *trust* you before they do business with you.

Your reputation matters now more than ever, and that can be a really scary thing for some of us. Think of it as though you are constantly job-hunting, and every conversation is a small interview. Yes, you need to be on your best behavior and, yes, you need to be genuine and caring. You don't know who people know, and, most importantly, you don't know how that may affect your business in the long term. Either by direct interaction or word of mouth, you could be losing opportunities.

When you own a business, you are a salesperson. And salespeople are the brand they are representing. The point is this: You are not separate from your company when you begin as an entrepreneur. Everything, from your logo to your mission statement, to the way your website looks and feels, needs to be consistent and be a brand that you, the *real* you, can live up to.

Of course, you can't mimic your brand all the time, but it's important that the big things are similar to how you present yourself. Here are some examples to get you thinking:

1. Clothing: Is your brand classic and clean-cut or relaxed and fun? How do your clothes support this?

2. Language: Is your brand voice elevated and educational or low-key and a fan of slang?

3. Networking: Are you often comfortable speaking to several people at once and are you continuously circling the room? (Your brand might be more assertive, aggressive.) Or are you against the wall, speaking to only one or two people at a time? (Your brand might be more reserved, quiet.)

Consider where you fall in each of these categories and that will help you match your business to your reputation. I'm not someone who walks into an event in red high heels, always with a new story about my last trip to Barbados on my lips (although that would be awesome). Therefore, because that's not me, my brand doesn't include bright colors like pink or red and I don't use many exclamation points in my marketing. I also keep nearly all my references to Charlotte, because that's where I do business. My brand is subtle, low-key, and local because that's who I am as a person.

BEAT IMPOSTER SYNDROME WITH SINCERITY

I was at a networking event once where the group had brought in some amazing speakers, not all of whom were entrepreneurs but who had an important story to tell, nonetheless. One of the speakers was a local news anchor who spoke of her escape from domestic abuse. You would never, in a hundred years, look at her and realize what she had been through. And that's the point, right? We think an ugly term like "abuse" has a specific face. It doesn't. It can affect anyone.

Her speech brought many people to tears, and I went up to her afterwards to thank her for her courage and for sharing such an important message. There was, rightfully so, a long line to chat with her. However, one woman caught my attention. She thanked the speaker, shook her hand, and then slipped the speaker her business card. Which was fine, except as she did so, she said, "If you ever need some event planning, just give me a call."

There's nothing wrong with marketing yourself, and, yes, you should try to pass out your business card as much as possible. But also: Read the room. Not every person you meet is an opportunity to gain new business, and certainly not after they've shared something so personal, even if it was shared in a public space. Sometimes, yes, you need to fake it to make business contacts, but, if at any point you come across as insincere, your credibility goes out the window. And not just with the person you were talking to, but with anyone who witnessed it as well.

In business, when you put yourself out there, you need to maintain the balance between fighting imposter syndrome and being sincere. The term "imposter syndrome" is defined as feeling inadequate despite contradictory evidence of great success.[9] It's very common that you will feel this at multiple stages in your entrepreneurial journey. And not feeling confident about your service, product, or even your ability to provide to your client what you are promising them is normal. That doesn't mean, however, that you can't also be sincere. Being sincere is about how you frame what you are saying. There's a difference between saying, "We can *definitely* help you," and making a promise you can't keep (insincere and possibly a lie), and saying, "We are going to do our best to make that happen for you," (sincere and more realistic).

When you are sincere and realistic about your business, you are actually helping yourself in the long run to beat imposter syndrome because you are beginning to establish a pattern of under-promising

---

[9] Corkindale, Gill. "Overcoming Imposter Syndrome." *Harvard Business Review*, 2 Dec. 2019, hbr.org/2008/05/overcoming-imposter-syndrome.

and over-delivering. True, a client might prefer to hear, "We can definitely help you," but then what happens if you aren't able to deliver? The client is disappointed and will most likely not work with you again. If you are sincere with them and truly doing your best to solve a problem for them, they will appreciate the effort, especially when you didn't make a promise you couldn't keep.

Gut check. None of us know what we're doing. The point is, you are going to learn a lot about your business while you are in the middle of doing the work. I often refer to this as building the plane while you're flying it. However, when you position yourself with sincerity, you give yourself the grace to find the solution *and* possibly not find a solution – because that's how real life will sometimes work out. Instead of feeding into your feelings of inadequacy, or imposter syndrome, this will instead become an opportunity where you build trust with a client.

In business, if people learn that your words are insincere, then they won't trust you, and if they don't trust you, they're not going to want to work with you, even if they can't name the exact reason why.

Some clients or partners might change their mind on whether they trust you so quickly that you won't even have time to blink. It's easy to do that in a world where we have as many options as we do when making purchasing decisions. The same is 100 per cent true of your industry. And when you're the new kid in town, it's going to take some time to build and maintain trust. Do you have specific brands that you always buy, even if another brand is on sale? Is there a friend you always go to for relationship advice and another who is always there for you for comedic relief? It's the same with business. People will find what niche you fill for them and vice versa. It will be hard to accomplish that if you give people an uncomfortable gut reaction.

The biggest driver of success for you and your business is this: **Be a real and decent human being**. People will know when you're not.

Strategies for Beating Imposter Syndrome

Some days, this will be easier than others. But as we've discussed, it's important to be sincere, even if it may not *seem* like something the client would want to hear. This is especially important when it comes to beating imposter syndrome, because the more honest and sincere you are about the reality of the work you can provide, the more likely you will, in fact, live up to that expectation.

Here are some questions you may be asked in your first year of business that you may not feel confident enough to answer. To beat imposter syndrome, practice your response to these questions in the mirror, in the car, or in the shower:

1. How long have you been doing this? *Talk about your experience generally, and then why you started your business.*

2. How many clients have you worked with in your industry? *Discuss the strategies you use to help clients and describe the type of clients you work with.*

3. Have you done this type of project before? *If you haven't, consider how your experience to date might be useful for this type of project. Talk about what you can do to benefit the client.*

Saying "No" and Still Being Sincere

Finally, there will be times when you will – without question – have to say "no." This will not ever be fun, but especially when you're in the first year of your business. However, that does not mean that you can't still be helpful and still make the sale. Part of being sincere is knowing when you *can't* do something, but still offering a solution.

For example, "I'm sorry, that's just not doable for your timeline and budget," is a very real phrase you will learn to say. But that shouldn't be the end of the conversation. You can be sincere and honest: "We can't do this for you because it's not possible in a short period of time or because it will require more manpower and more money," while still providing support: "However, here is what we can do for your timeline and your budget." Always offer a solution. Some clients might truly not know how long a process takes or how much something should cost (and some may be trying to take advantage of you, but we'll talk more about that in Chapter 7). Regardless of their intention, it places you in the powerful position of being a professional, valuable resource.

There are a lot of things you won't be able to control when owning a business, but your promises and the customer service you provide at the end of the day should absolutely be in your control. You can choose to be insincere and promise things you may or may not be able to deliver, or you can choose to be sincere and know your limits. There is always time to Google it later or offer alternative solutions. It doesn't make you a failure or "imposter" in your field. It makes you a real person and – most of all – a professional. The right clients will see that.

End-of-Chapter Check-in

EXERCISE 1: FIND OUT WHO YOU ARE

Keep in mind that there is no "wrong" type of personality when it comes to owning a business. However, there are definitely areas where you might need to adapt differently in order to be successful. List at least five personality traits that may need to be adapted for networking and your sales process. (The first one is done as an example.)

1. Trait 1: Extrovert
   a. Hurdle: Might talk more than the client and not hear their problem/need
   b. Adaptation: Practice ending a story or anecdote with a thoughtful question

2. Trait 2: _____
   a. Hurdle:
   b. Adaptation:

3. Trait 3: _____
   a. Hurdle:
   b. Adaptation:

4. Trait 4: _____
   a. Hurdle:
   b. Adaptation:

EXERCISE 2: YOUR BRAND REPUTATION

How would you describe yourself in these three areas? Then, how would you translate this to your business?

1. Clothing: What are you most comfortable wearing?
2. Language: What are some familiar phrases you say throughout the day that would be comforting (and appropriate) for work?
3. Networking: How do you comfortably navigate larger events? What does this say about how your business should be seen by the public?

EXERCISE 3: BEATING IMPOSTER SYNDROME WITH SINCERITY

A client has just asked you to complete a task that you don't know how to do. Brainstorm two ways you can respond positively without saying "no" (because you're going to Google it later).

Then, brainstorm two ways you can positively say "no" (because you know for a fact you can't get it done). After, offer two alternative solutions. (For example: Unfortunately, we can't do that, but this is what we can do...)

6

Get to Know Other People

B efore becoming an entrepreneur, I thought networking was useful only when you were ready to make a career change. You needed to make some contacts, test the waters, and see what was out there. The best way to do that would be to go to an uncomfortable networking event with a bunch of strangers, swapping business cards and giving your elevator pitch over and over again until someone said, "Great! I want to work with you."

Turns out, I was wrong about all of this (thank goodness). Networking is actually being in the right rooms with the right people. And very often, you are going to need to meet several people before the right person invites you into the right room. This happened at the very beginning of my business. I was just under two months in when I reached out to a contact I had made at my previous job. He and I were from the same hometown and had gone to the same alma mater, which was a little unique since our college was out of state. He was in marketing as well, but at a very large agency. He was not going to be a client of mine. In fact, technically, you could say he was a competitor, except that he wasn't, since his agency had a staff of over 100 and I had literally only seven weeks under my belt.

He invited me to a networking breakfast, and he told me of a contact who would likely be a good referral source for me, who would also be at the breakfast. To this day, I remember this introduction. Did I give my elevator pitch? Poorly. Did we follow up with coffee? We did. We also followed up with a few more lunches, coffees, and impromptu "Hey, I need some advice" meetings. Has that person been a wonderful referral source? Absolutely. Did it take more than my elevator pitch to secure that relationship? It sure did. I knew that our first introduction to each other would be important, but what was more important was what came after: the conversation, the follow-up, and eventually the referral of business.

When you're an entrepreneur, networking events become the lifeblood of your business. They're also a wonderful place to make friends. Networking is important, but it can also be complex. Here are a few topics we should cover:

1. How to network effectively
2. The types of people you'll meet
3. Client project partnerships
4. The bright side of networking
5. The darker side of networking

HOW TO NETWORK EFFECTIVELY

Networking effectively is very important. But it also takes some time to find the right networking group. It's likely that you won't know where your network is going to evolve until you try out a few events and groups. For example, I kept up with one of my non-profit networking groups when I started my business even though I didn't think it would be a good referral source for me. I kept going because I enjoyed the company, and I often learned something new whenever I went. Good thing I did keep going, because one of the people in that group ended up referring me to one of their clients who was looking for a social media manager. That client ended up being one of my biggest contracts in the beginning of growing my business. So, even if you don't think a group will refer you a lot of business, if you enjoy the company, and gain something from being there, it's important still to go. You never know what surprising business might result.

To network effectively, you'll want to:
1. Find a good networking group
2. Schedule networking into your planner

Find a Good Networking Group

To find a good networking group, you could just throw a bunch of events on your calendar and tackle them all until you find a good group. But that would be as sane as test-driving every car at a dealership until you find one that fits all your needs. You need to have some forethought and do your research. To find a good networking group, you should:

1. Know the basic characteristics of a good networking group
2. Research the people in the group
3. Understand the difference between national and local networking groups
4. Know how to find good networking groups online

The Basic Characteristics of a Good Networking Group

Finding a good networking group is similar to dating. Yes, it's a numbers game (the more groups you attend, the higher your chance of finding the right fit), but it's also about finding the right group for the right time in your business. What you consider a good networking group will evolve as your business grows. For example, in the beginning, you may need a networking group that is full of like-minded individuals also starting out on their entrepreneurial journey. As your business grows, you may begin to branch out into more mature and industry-focused networking groups because that's where you know your clients will be. Regardless of the stage you are in, there are a few things you need to keep in mind. Any good networking group should:

✓ Be a group that connects businesspeople looking to grow professionally. Some of the members may own businesses, and some may not.

✓ Have some type of fee to join (but almost always allow you to visit at least once for free). Keep in mind, a fee doesn't necessarily make it "better," but it does usually mean that the people who show up to the event are a little more serious. Think about it: If you get very busy at work, is it easy to bail on an event that didn't cost you anything? Sure. Now, if you paid forty-five dollars for that lunch, you might pause before choosing not to show up.

✓ Be made up of people who are or who work with your ideal client, because the group is only as good as the people in it. So, consider your ideal client: Think about who they are and, more importantly, whom they work with. Chances are, the people in this group are not the ones you'll do business with – but they will give you access to their networks, which should include your ideal client.

Keep in mind, too, that some networking groups have rules. They may require that you refer a certain amount of business to other members or that you attend a certain number of events, for example. These are the rules for being a member of the group, so do your research and make sure that you're comfortable with them when deciding whether or not to join.

Research the People in the Group

Here's when being a stalker is a good thing. Most networking web-sites should have a member directory. If not, it's possible they have a Facebook Group or Page. That said, if you really work at it and still can't find out anything about their members, that doesn't necessarily mean that they aren't a good group for you to join. (It could just mean marketing is not their strongest asset.) Regardless, if you're feeling anxious about attending a group for the first time without knowing anyone there, see if you can connect with one of their head officers. Either the president or vice president should, at the very least, be listed on their website. Often, those members will be glad to network with you one on one and tell you more about the group, if you ask.

If you don't know anyone in the group, or can't find out anything about the members, all is not lost. Virtual groups will sometimes send out an attendee list ahead of time for people to connect with each other. And some in-person groups will list their attendees on the event page, which you can see after you sign up. Stick to the free events in these instances. You don't want to pay for an event and then see that their member list isn't helpful for your business.

As you look at these lists, remember that you are not necessarily looking for people who will be ideal clients for you. People at these events might be, sure. But you should primarily be looking for people who are good referral partners. They know the people you need to know. For example, since I work with businesses that are at that "next page" of their marketing plan, many of my referral partners are, naturally, business coaches. Business coaches work with a variety of industries.and provide advice to their clients on how to implement the next steps of their business plans. Marketing is often a part of that discussion.

The Difference Between National and Local Networking Groups

There are some major national groups out there, such as Ellevate, AMA (American Marketing Association), NAWBO (National

Association of Women Business Owners), and so on, but those are all subject to your local chapters. Just because one AMA chapter in Chicago is great, that doesn't mean that the chapter in St. Louis is as good. (Heck, two AMA chapters in the same zip code could be widely different.) So, do your research.

There are also a ton of local groups that were started by people frustrated with the limitations and rules of national organizations. These local groups operate within their own rules, which can be good or bad, depending on how like-minded you are with the leadership. They will also likely have a tighter fit with the local business community, since the group would have been built by locals. Obviously, one drawback will be their resources and reach, which will likely remain within your town or city. There aren't going to be big conventions in New York City or a nationwide database for you to pull from when you need resources. However, I've found that these small local groups are where I have made some of my closest friends in business. And those friendships have extended beyond our mutual support of each other's work.

How to Find Good Networking Groups Online

You can succeed at online networking if you know what to look for. Here's how you do it. First, keep it to groups where you know someone else in the "virtual" room who can introduce you, either on camera to the rest of the group or in the chat box. Also, look for groups that mention "breakout rooms." This is important. This means that there will be a point during the event where the host will "break" everyone into groups, digitally. Your screen will change to that smaller, specific group of people and allow for more one-on-one discussion. Dedicated time spent with a smaller group of five to ten people increases your chances of making a connection with (at least) one of them. I would also recommend that you stick to local groups when it comes to virtual networking. This way, you'll be able to follow up in person, increasing the chances that you'll develop a productive business relationship with them.

National virtual groups are also an option. I would always recommend that if you are interested in the topic, then join the group. However, with hundreds of viewers across the country tuning in for a virtual event, it's unlikely that you'll make the right connections unless they provide breakout rooms as part of the event.

Schedule Networking into Your Planner

I remember the first official day of being on my own. I had scheduled an early morning networking event. Afterward, I posted up at a coffee shop and began combing through my planner. Days and weeks (and months) stretched ahead of me in those blank, white pages, and no one was going to fill them except for me. So, I made that my mission. Meet people. Talk to people. Go to events. Get out there. At first, I wasn't discerning. I didn't know what I didn't know. What I *did* know was that blank space on my calendar was not good. That's when I, over the course of one cup of coffee, stopped being shy about asking people for meetings, started researching groups I had never heard of, and found as many work-related opportunities as possible available to me within a twenty-five-mile radius.

Here are some tips to get you started when you first begin filling up your calendar:

1. Reach out to your immediate business network: people you have worked with, people you have worked for, and close connections at other companies.

2. Use LinkedIn to search for valuable connections. Who is currently working in your industry? Who is a 1st connection already? Who is a 2nd connection, but you know someone who can introduce you to them?

3. Research events that sound promising in terms of networking or that appear educational. MeetUp, Eventbrite, and Facebook are good places to start.

THE TYPES OF PEOPLE YOU'LL MEET

In March 2020, COVID-19 swept through nations and overwhelmed our healthcare systems, creating the first pandemic that many of us had experienced in our lives. About four days before the mandated lockdown in Mecklenburg County, North Carolina, where I live, my grandmother unexpectedly ended up in the emergency room with back pain. She had just turned ninety-four and we had believed her to be healthier than most of us. What we had thought was a pulled muscle turned out to be cancer that had spread throughout her body. Within twenty-four hours, she was in hospice care.

As emotionally traumatic as it was for me and my family members to wrap our minds around my grandmother's very sharp decline, we were racing against the clock to get my sister and two uncles to Charlotte to see my grandmother and say their goodbyes before the hospital forbid any visitors from entering the building. At this time, there were very few answers, and my parents and I were up most of the night anxiously worrying about who would get to the airport, and what the fastest route would be to get them to the hospital to see my grandmother.

I turned to my network for help. I reached out to a few close friends who just so happened to be professional partners, and even to my clients to see if they had any connections within the healthcare system in Charlotte. And, in an act very unlike me, I reached out to a networking group where I only knew a handful of the people very well. I'm a private person by nature. The group had close to 600 members on their Facebook page, so I wasn't comfortable with it, but I needed help. I posted on the page about my family's situation, asking if anyone could connect us with the right hospice staff (or anyone, really) to make sure someone would be with my grandmother when she passed.

The leader of this group (she's a leader for a reason) reached out. She had recently connected with the CEO of this hospital system on LinkedIn.

"I've never met him," she said. "We just became connected. I'm glad to reach out if it'll help."

I thanked her and answered, "Yes, please do."

A few hours later, she had a reply which she forwarded to me. I couldn't believe it. In the middle of a pandemic, the CEO of a hospital system had given an answer to someone he didn't know, about a family that was worried about someone who could just have been "another patient." He gave us a clear answer on what the rules were (we would be allowed to be with my grandmother, just two at a time) and where we should go if we had any issues.

I couldn't thank her enough. She didn't know my family. She didn't know the CEO. But despite all that, she'd made a connection and helped where she could. It wasn't about business. It wasn't about making money. It was about more than that. When I told her how much it meant to my family and how my dad was eternally grateful, she simply responded, "Tell him his daughter would have done the same for me."

There are some pretty amazing people you can meet when you own a business. You can make like-minded friends, meet potential partners, get clients, and much, much more.

Although this can, of course, take some time. At first, you may have no idea what type of people you'll meet at any one event. But it's important to know what categories they fall into and how to connect with them. Here's how I look at it. The people you'll meet are:

1. "Pens" and "Pencils"
2. People in your referral network

"Pens" and "Pencils"

I met a lot of people during my first year in business, and a major lesson I took away from all those meetings was this: If you're in the right city (and I hope you are), you are going to find your people very quickly, and they will welcome you with open arms. By your people, I mean people within the same entrepreneurial space as you. Potential referral partners, prospective clients, and people who will become part of your support systems.

Regardless of whether you're in the right city or not, you will – without a doubt – come across people who are only partially dipping their toe in entrepreneurship and who, therefore, cannot take you seriously because they don't take the concept of business-owning seriously. And you will also come across people who scrambled so quickly to get to the top of whatever field they are in that they've forgotten (or have chosen to block out) what it was like to crawl and beg, desperately asking people for a coffee or an introduction.

On the whole, when I was meeting someone "blind" for the first time, I could usually place them into one of these categories:

- **The Pen:** This is the person who has taken the time to build, cultivate, and check in with their business relationships. They know who a good contact is, and they genuinely want to help if they can. They are not temporary contacts. They are more permanent, and they do what they say they will do.

- **The Pencil:** This is the person who is temporary. They're only half involved in the conversation unless there's something in it for them. They erase people very quickly, even if some of those people might have been helpful to them in the future. Sometimes, they're trying to erase those people in the middle of a conversation. You know who they are. They're checking their phone while they're talking to you, or you can hear them typing while you're asking them a question over the phone. You can't rely on them.

Now that I've called them out, you'll recognize these people immediately. Sometimes, though, pencils can act like pens at first, and there are pens whose business success causes them to become pencils. I'd like to believe that I'm a pen ninety-nine per cent of the time. But there have been days, or hours, when I am barely even a pencil. Don't feel as though you need to be a pen right away – you'll get there. But where you can, give back. Provide contact information or simply mail (yes, actually mail) a thank you note, especially if you know that person *is* a pen. It'll do wonders for your networking in the future.

People in Your Referral Network

Your referral network will very likely be the spine of your business, whether you're B2B or B2C – at least in the beginning. A referral network is a group of people who will, like the name suggests, refer you business. This group could be made up of people you pinpoint and vet through networking groups or current/past clients. It could also include friends and family. Don't be ashamed of using your personal connections to market yourself. Those who love you will be more than happy to support you or spread the word in any way they can.

> **There are three types of people you will accrue in your referral network:**
> 1. Business partners
> 2. Clients
> 3. Friends and family

Business Partners

Partners in business are a lot like partners in real life. You're looking for someone who shares the same values and work ethic as you, and whom you like as a person. There's a saying from the speaker Jim Rohn, "You are the average of the five people you spend the most time with." I remember this often when I invite someone into my circle. Choose your business partners wisely.

Soon enough, you will come to understand what characteristics you're looking for in a good referral partner. What you'll want to remember, as you start making referral partners, is that what goes around comes around. I learned this early on. When I first started out, I realized that there were a lot of people out there to work with who did not need or were not ready for my services – but that didn't mean I couldn't refer them to someone else I knew for the other services they needed. And those people could then refer the client to others in their network. This came around full circle for me when my connections began referring work back to me. They might say,

"Hey Cassandra, thank you so much for that contact. We've created her website and she's now ready to tackle her social media, so I'm going to send her back to you." It may not *always* come back around full circle, but I truly believe (because I've seen it) that the more you give to your referral network, the more you will get something back.

Take a look at the lists below, and keep this in mind as you start networking and growing your business. This will help you decide whether or not to make a connection with a partner.

Good Partners Will...	Good Partners Will NOT...
Include you on introductory calls/meetings with a prospect.	Forget to "upsell" your service to a prospect or client.
Keep several of your business cards to give out on your behalf.	Ask you to hand out their business cards without returning the favor.
Be mindful of your schedule and check in for lunch or coffee once a quarter or every other quarter.	Ask for calls, meetings, lunches, and so on regularly, but which result in conversations that are not fruitful.
Keep you in the loop on upcoming networking events that may be of benefit to you.	Reach out only to promote their own webinars or events (especially when there is a hefty cost associated with it).
Introduce you to other potential partners/clients via email or in person.	Mention someone who would be a good fit for you, and then never follow up by making an introduction.

THIS WON'T BE PRETTY

Clients

Happy clients are a great referral source for you. They know intimately how you work and the type of deliverable you will provide. Furthermore, they know people in *their* network (their business partners, clients, and friends) who could use your services. Someone in your client's network is one of the warmest leads you can get, so don't be shy about asking a happy client if they know anyone else who might need what you do. They might not, and that's okay – because you can always ask later. Even if a client moves on after a project is complete, as long as you parted on positive terms, it would be totally normal for you to reach out a few months later to say hello and see how they are. Once you've reopened the line of communication, you can share information on any new services you're offering or products you're working on. Without needing to "sell" yourself, you can let them know what type of clients you're looking for, and that they should feel free to share your information with anyone who fits that profile. This happens all the time in business, and good referral partners will be happy to do it.

Friends and Family

There's a funny scene in the TV show "Schitt's Creek" where the son, David, opens a new business and offers his parents a "friends and family discount of twenty per cent." His father, played by the great Eugene Levy, asks, "If your mother and I purchase something together, does that mean we would get a forty per cent discount?" David replies, exasperated, "Why would you want to spend *less* money at my store?"

I know this feeling all too well. Not only have I done "pro-bono" work for some family members (to be fair, Dad paid for four years of college, so I guess we're even), but I've also had some friends "jokingly" complain about my prices when I send them an invoice, even if I've discounted my services significantly.

Having a "friends and family" discount is a great perk for people close to you who do business with you. However, having friends and family who expect you to give away your services for next to nothing (or for forty per cent off) is like walking a tightrope. That's why I would recommend that the best way for your friends and family to support you is for them to help get your name out there – to tell *their* friends and family about your business. They can do this very easily through social media by liking, commenting, and sharing the content you are pushing out.

And if they happen to know someone who sounds like they might need a service you provide, they will certainly be a huge champion for you (or should be). Don't worry, though; you won't have to arm your relatives and friends with your elevator pitch or a list of your services. Instead, you can simply invite them to follow you on social media or connect with you on LinkedIn. And, especially with the people you are closest to, consider giving them some of your business cards. They'll likely be proud to pass out your business cards and share any other information they have about your business with people they know.

CLIENT PROJECT PARTNERSHIPS

In addition to knowing what kinds of people might be included in your referral network, you also need to know what kinds of people you might end up partnering with for a client project.

A client project partnership is a relationship where you work with another company to complete work promised to a client. These are important because, as we've discussed, you can't be all things to all people. However, that doesn't mean you can't deliver specific asks *if* you have the right partnerships in place. You will likely meet these people through your networking circles, but it's also reasonable for you to reach out on LinkedIn and Facebook (particularly business Facebook groups) and ask for referrals to people/businesses that provide a specific service.

These may be people in your industry, or these may be people in different industries. There are a lot of ways you can set up these client project partnerships. Here are the different options available to you:

White Label: In this kind of client project partnership, your partner brings you on to do uncredited work for a client of theirs. Your company basically doesn't exist, but your work does. You simply do the work, then give it to your partner, who will then claim it as their own when communicating with their client. Don't panic – this is completely normal in this kind of partnership, and it's understood that you won't get credit for your work. In terms of working with your partner's client, you usually don't have direct access, but, if you do, you act as though you are your partner's employee. White Label partnerships can provide you with good, steady work and I have definitely been a part of (and continue to be part of) partnerships like this.

Referral Fee: In this client project partnership, you receive an agreed-upon amount for referring a client to your partner (often, this amount is a percentage of the project/contract fee). Your partner also refers clients to you using the same arrangement. However, depending on the type of service you are providing, this amount may look slightly different. For example, "smaller" (here, smaller refers to the cost) services and/or products would result in a smaller referral fee, and would likely be a one-time event per each referral. However, for larger projects, for example, a website, it would be reasonable to ask for a small percentage of the overall project with half of the payment at the start of the project and the rest once the project is complete.

Good Faith: This is a reciprocal relationship you build over time with a partner, where the both of you share work with each other as mutually as possible. This kind of client project partnership is most effective when one of you brings in the other to work together on a big project. For example, if I were helping a client rebrand their messaging, I would bring in a partner who did logo design. Vice versa, this designer partner would bring me in for brand messaging when a client came to her for a rebrand.

THE BRIGHT SIDE OF NETWORKING

The most important lesson I've learned from networking is that everybody has something to offer, even if you don't think their industry is a fit for you. I've met with information technology specialists, credit card merchant providers, and more financial advisors than I will ever need to know in one lifetime. I know enough about their services to refer clients to them, but, more importantly, I know a little about them personally, too, so if or when I run into them again, I'll be able to ask them how they are doing – and mean it. This not only helps build sincerity, which we discussed in the last chapter, but also builds trust, which is incredibly important to gaining and maintaining clients that might come from their networks.

THE DARKER SIDE OF NETWORKING

Very early on in running my business, I was at a networking group where I met a woman who was obviously uncomfortable with me visiting the group. "Well, I do that," she said after I explained my business to her. So, I explained further, in an attempt to demonstrate how my services were different from hers. "Yes, I do that, too!" she said, irritated. As our conversation continued, it seemed that she was convinced she offered every single service available in the marketing industry – implying that there was no room for me in her networking group. The thing is, though, you can't do all aspects of any one industry. Even if she claimed she did every marketing service that existed, there was no way she did them all well. Not by herself, at least. If you're going to be the person who does all the things, without a niche, it's going to be really tough to build your network and keep your clients happy. Not sharing the pie with someone else in your industry is, first of all, arrogant, but, second of all, bad karma. Because what goes around comes around. Literally.

Now, there are some networking groups who will only allow one member per industry, but even then, there is often wiggle room. For example, a family law attorney is not going to compete with an estate attorney necessarily, but they may be great referral sources for one another. The best networking groups will allow for some overlap in any one industry, and those who know their niche will work well with others in that group.

There are many challenges you'll face when networking, and not all are about your business. It's important to know what those are and how to overcome them. These include:

1. When people jump to conclusions about you
2. When people are (this is a reality for us, ladies) sexist toward you

When People Jump to Conclusions About You

Here's the thing: Meeting people you don't know can suck even if you like meeting people, because the odds are that there are going to be some weird and awkward interactions when you're networking. That can come with added layers if you're A) young, B) anything other than a straight male, or C) any race other than white. Some stereotypes still reign. I can only speak to my experience in Charlotte,

North Carolina (a fairly progressive city in the South), but chances are – no matter who you are or where you live – you're going to come across some non-professional situations where people jump to conclusions about you because of stereotypes they subscribe to.

Some interactions are funny, like when a woman I was meeting with to discuss a potential partnership ended up telling me way too much personal information about her new marriage. She did this because she subscribed to the stereotype that women always share the intimate details of their personal lives with each other. "*I just wanted to discuss this potential partnership*," I felt like screaming through the smile plastered on my face. "*Okay, it's great that your sex life is so awesome, but maybe you're sharing a bit too much, considering that I've known you for only twelve minutes.*"

For better or for worse, you bring yourself to the table when you represent your company. And there are a lot of things that can cause the person sitting across the table from you to make a snap judgment about or jump to a conclusion about you. This is true for all of us. Some examples of what might cause them to do this include:

- You look young
- You look old
- You appear single (no wedding ring)
- You appear married, or to have kids
- Your skin is a different shade
- You have a hearing aid
- You have a speech impediment

People jump to conclusions because it's part of being human. Why? Because biases do exist, and you have more than likely experienced this at the very least as a woman, and possibly for other reasons listed above.

Certain people will subscribe to specific stereotypes. If they hear a stereotype enough, either from acquaintances or from society as a whole, they'll begin to believe it even if they aren't doing so consciously. This is called systemic bias. And when you're battling centuries of systemic biases present in our culture, you can't expect to win the war in an afternoon coffee meeting. Unfortunately, some people will inevitably jump to conclusions about you. But there are strategies to help protect your emotional well-being, especially since you never quite know when the dark side of networking will rear its ugly head.

What to Do When People Jump to Conclusions About You

I'll admit, when it came to writing this portion of my book, I felt woefully inadequate to provide helpful strategies for when people jump to conclusions about you. Because when it happens, you're likely going to feel shocked and upset. And if you're like me, you're going to get very angry. All of these emotions are valid, but they don't necessarily help you navigate this situation. So, I've enlisted the help of a dear friend, Dr. Nicole French, who is a clinical psychologist and, therefore, much better suited to providing strategies that will serve you.

The first strategy Dr. French recommends is to pause. (Pausing, by the way, is a good idea no matter what hurdle you are facing in your business.) Then, once you've taken a moment to pause, notice how you feel. Here are some different feelings you may be experiencing:

1. I want to disappear/escape (flee)
2. I want to explain, correct, or justify (fight)
3. I don't know what to do; I'm stuck (freeze)
4. I want to pretend this isn't happening (faint)

By first acknowledging how you feel, you bring your attention inward, which is where you should direct your energy. Whether you want to fight, freeze, or just run away from the situation, it's important to calm yourself down once you've identified your feelings. Dr. French recommends naming your emotion, by saying to yourself, "I am suffering right now. I feel [name emotion]." From here, practice deep breathing, even though it may be very difficult if you've been triggered. If you can bring your breath back to your body and focus on the one thing you can control, you are directing yourself toward the person who needs your attention most: you.

Here are some helpful responses that Dr. French recommends if you feel that you are being judged in one of these areas.

- **You look young (ageism):** I hear that my youth causes you to doubt whether I am the right person to do this work for you. I have full confidence in my skillset, and I have experience that will inform this work. I understand that you are exploring options, and I would be happy to discuss concerns about competence or experience if that will help us determine how to proceed.

- **You look old (ageism):** I hear that my age causes you to doubt whether I am the right person to do this work for you. For me, age has gifted me with wisdom and experience that richly inform my life and my work. I understand that you are exploring options, and I would be happy to discuss what concerns come up for you in regard to my age.

- **You appear single (no wedding ring):** I'm curious to learn more about how you see [my relationship status] impacting or informing our work together.

- **You appear married, or to have kids:** I'm curious about your preferences regarding marital or parental status with respect to finding a good fit for this project.

- **Your skin is a different shade (racism):** How do you think the color of my skin will impact the work we may do together?

- **You have a hearing aid (ableism):** I've learned to use the supports available that enable me to not lose my edge and to contribute in the ways I am meant to. This support, while not fashionable, enables me to connect meaningfully using all my senses. I'm curious to know if you think it has impacted our communication.

- **You have a speech impediment (ableism):** I've learned to adapt and/or I'm learning how to adapt. How does my speech influence our communication?

Although it's much easier to remember these replies in moments of calm, having some talking points available and practicing calming your nervous system could very well turn an uncomfortable situation into a learning opportunity for the person on the other side of the table.

You may have noticed a theme in these responses: If you have the emotional capacity in the moment, put the onus back on the other person. When you state that you are curious about their feelings, it invites the other person to engage in a (hopefully) helpful dialogue that reveals a misunderstanding or an implicit bias of which they are not aware. However.

Not all of us are able to maintain a clear head and provide a logical, "teachable" response when we are triggered. I know in many situations like this, I am tongue-tied and simply unwilling to engage in further conversation with the person. Ending the conversation and walking away is one hundred per cent acceptable. A simple "Thank you for your time, but I have another meeting to get to," should do it without encouraging further dialogue. When we are triggered and feel the "fight, flight, flee or faint" response, it is our brain's way of protecting us. Do what you need to survive the moment.

Here are some additional tips from me when you encounter this darker side of networking:

- **Remember that the people in your circle change**: If you do meet someone who jumps to conclusions about you, remember that the biggest (and best) difference between working for yourself and working for someone else is that, when you work for yourself, the people who weave in and out of your circle will change quicker than the tides. Some will stay and become long-term partners and clients. Others will drift back outside of your circle and you may or may not run into them again. You can choose who stays and who goes.

- **You can keep conversations short**: To avoid having long conversations with people who've made assumptions about me, I've found that it helps to keep my business conversations short, with first meetings lasting forty-five minutes at the most. If things are really great between us, we can always follow up at a later time.

- **Trust your gut:** I feel like this tactic becomes easier with age (at least, it has for me). You know yourself best, and even if your brain or heart might be trying to convince you otherwise about a person, if you feel uncomfortable when speaking with someone but you can't put your finger on it – then it's okay not to follow up with them again.

When People Are Sexist Toward You

Let me tell you a story.

I once met a man for a get-to-know-you coffee.

For context, I should explain that, in these kinds of meetings, I allow the other person to do most of the talking up front so I can learn about their business and how we can work together. In a forty-five-minute meeting, I usually give twenty to thirty minutes to the person across the table, and then I'll talk about my business and how I may be able to help them. Meetings of this kind often have this structure, so when one of the people in the meeting isn't talking as much as they should be or is talking way too much, it's a red flag that's something's off with the conversation.

That's what happened at this meeting. We were at the one hour and ten-minute mark, and I hadn't yet said one word about my business. This man, let's call him George, talked. A lot. He was a business coach, and, as I've stated previously, business coaches are usually good referral sources for me. But I couldn't grasp who his clients were. I couldn't break in to ask a question to guide him toward a relatable topic. Even when I opened my mouth during a brief pause, he suddenly moved on to a whole new topic.

At this point, I was already doing that thing people do with their bodies when they aren't engaged in a conversation – turning their legs away from the person who's talking. I was practically sitting horizontally in my chair, and I kept shifting against the uncomfortable, wooden seat.

Well, *finally*, the topic changed. But not to one of the topics I had hoped for.

"I notice you don't have a wedding ring," he said, looking down at my left hand folded in my lap.

My eyes narrowed. There was no way this was going to end well. I didn't respond.

"Let me tell you why that is," he said, leaning forward.

I began clenching my fist, feeling as though I had to be prepared to punch him in the throat.

"There are just no good guys out there," he said. "Men don't know how to treat a woman these days, and it's becoming increasingly difficult for women to find safe, loving relationships."

I am very confident that my face read: *What the hell are you talking about? And how do you think this is appropriate right now?*

I quickly interjected that I had, in fact, been married, but that doing so again wasn't a priority for me right now. Usually, dropping the divorce card on the table shuts people up when they're trying to pry into your personal life. It scares them for some reason, so it's really useful for when strangers cross a line.

"I'm very sorry to hear that," he said, furrowing his brow. "That must be very difficult, especially for a woman in her thirties like you. Because, you know," he said, leaning forward again, as if sharing a secret with me, "all women are built to have children."

Now I was definitely going to punch him in the throat. I began to pick up my purse. We had reached the end of our conversation, and not only had he insulted me and pried into my personal life, but he had also wasted my time. If nothing else, *that* was unforgivable.

There were a lot of things I wanted to say to him at that moment. Looking back, perhaps I should have said them. It would have been worth the loss of the connection because – big surprise – he did not end up connecting me with an organization that needed my services. Instead of saying anything, though, I pulled my purse onto my shoulder and took my keys out of the inside pocket, the pepper spray canister dangling from the chain, begging me to use it. I was clenching my jaw and digging my toes into the insoles of my heels.

"Well, I appreciate your time this morning," I lied, "but I have an early lunch north of the city," I added, lying again. "So, I need to go."

"Oh! Oh, no. Okay." He stood up to shake my hand. "Next time I'm going to let you do all the talking," he said. "I talked way too much today!"

Nope. No next time.

What to Do When People are Sexist Toward You
My friend Dr. French knew of this story before I asked her to provide professional advice for this book on how to approach this kind of scenario. "What should I have done," I asked her, after the event first happened, "other than punch him in the face?" Her gentle response was, "That's an option. But it may result in natural consequences harmful to both parties."

Fine, fine.

Dr. French recommends acknowledging your feelings when assaulted with this type of behavior, just like she did in the prior section. These feelings might include: *Do I want to escape (flee)? Do I want to explain (fight)? Do I want to disappear (faint)? I don't know what to do (freeze)!*

It's also important to be self-compassionate in moments like this. Dr. French reminds us that it's important to state, "I am suffering," and, in this particular moment, to also remind yourself: "Many women are suffering or have suffered due to this behavior." Although it doesn't change what's happening, it does center your energy toward your emotions and taking care of what is arising for you. By actually doing this – *naming your emotion* – you trigger a release of chemicals in your brain that activate self-soothing. The researcher Dan Siegel calls this process "name it to tame it,"[10] and it works very well when you feel that your nervous system has been assaulted.

Dr. French also provides some options on how you can professionally end the topic at hand and steer the conversation back to the reason you are there (business), should you decide to stay at the table:

- It appears that my relationship status causes you worry. I appreciate your concern for me.

- I'm grateful to live in a time where marriage and/or motherhood for women is not necessary for survival, happiness, or security.

---

[10] Siegel, Dan. *The Whole-Brain Child: 12 Revolutionary Strategies to Nurture Your Child's Developing Mind.* Bantam, 2012.

- May we all engage in and prioritize practices that cultivate Love in all of its forms! I'm focused on that, and I hope you are, too.

How the person across the table responds to these close-ended comments will give you the information you need to decide whether you want to continue the conversation with them – let alone take them on as a client or business partner.

I also learned two lessons from this experience, which have made it easier for me to deal with sexism when I come across it as a female entrepreneur.

The first I learned from my business coach at the time this event occurred. After I relayed this story to him, he provided me with the lesson that I had to separate my business from my identity – a lesson that I'd never realized I needed to learn. And yet, it's a common problem. It's probably something most entrepreneurs struggle with – the inability to separate their personal and business lives. After all, it feels like our businesses *are* personal. We give a lot of ourselves to them. Even my business name and logo scream Cassandra. How could I separate the identity of my business and the identity of myself?

"This is how," my business coach told me:

"Your business is an extension of your identity. Clients cannot – not ever – touch you as a person. Who you are as a person, your thoughts, values, dreams, and fears – they cannot touch that. They never have

access to that. Just remember that when you are sitting in front of people."

It may seem like a subtle mental shift – and it is – but it really helped me going forward. Later, when I faced sexist situations, like when I had a meeting with what I'd thought was a promising prospect and instead was propositioned for a date, I chose not to take it personally. I was hurt, but they had only grazed the surface. They had not touched me, the real me. Then I'd vent to someone who loved me and take a deep breath. Tomorrow was a clean slate.

The second lesson this experience taught me was that I really pride myself on being a female entrepreneur, whatever the challenges that come with it. It's a big part of my identity. And I use it all the time when networking and reaching out to other female entrepreneurs for collaboration.

I enjoy meeting all people in my industry – other marketing professionals, strategists, and creatives – but I especially enjoy meeting women who, like me, took a chance and left a stable career to pursue something more. Once when I was speaking with another female entrepreneur, she said something that made me pause: "Why do we have to be female entrepreneurs? Why aren't we just entrepreneurs? There's no such thing as a male entrepreneur." *Hmm.* I was labeled as a female entrepreneur, and I furthered that story by promoting myself proudly as a "female-owned and operated agency."

However, I think it's important to embrace this identity. It took me a long time to become a confident woman, and to build a support system around me of people who encouraged me to use that confidence and not be ashamed of it. It's that confidence that provided me with the platform I needed to start my own business – and to know in my bones that it was the right decision. Finding my strength as a woman is an important part of my story. In turn, I want to share that story and support other women in finding and using their voices in ways that make them feel equally confident and happy. I want to share whatever I can with whomever I can – in the same way other women have done for me.

Do I want the word "female" to be attached to my identity? I think so. It's more than just an adjective. It's an important part of my story. It tells you about my strength. And it's a badge of honor.

A Fun Fact for Female Entrepreneurs

If you're a small business owner *and* a woman, you have a lot of opportunities to work with state and government businesses. Many states require that their departments outsource to diverse businesses, and if your business is female-owned and small, you automatically qualify. A quick Google search in your county and state can determine what options are available to you. And if you have a business coach or accountant in your network, buy them some coffee. Pick their brain. They will likely be able to help you take the next steps in securing this badge of honor.

End-of-Chapter Check-In

EXERCISE 1: HOW TO NETWORK EFFECTIVELY

1. Determine what the best time is for you to meet people and grow your network. Most events happen in the morning before corporate jobs begin (7:30 a.m.), at lunch (11:30 a.m.), or after work (5:30 p.m.). If you have flexibility, determine what is best for your personality. For example, if you're a morning person and not a night owl, you'll want to stick to those morning meetings.

2. Find four networking events in the upcoming month that include different types of people so you can get a feel for what kind of group is the best fit for you. If they have a fee attached, sign up. This way, it's harder to back out later if you get cold feet.

3. When you go to these networking events, identify any leads that you should follow up. Also, identify all contacts, so that, later on, when you inevitably shift some of your business strategy, you can revisit the possibility of contacting them if necessary. Use the chart below to do this.

Before Networking		After Networking			
Event Name	Time	No. of Leads	Possible Referral Partners? (Follow up with coffee)	Possible Client Project Partners? (Follow up with coffee)	LinkedIn Contact Only (Connect, no need to follow up right now)

EXERCISE 2: THE TYPES OF PEOPLE YOU'LL MEET

1. Ask yourself what businesses complement, but don't compete with, your business. How can you partner with the contacts running these businesses and share resources?

   Example: Website design was not making me any money (and I disliked it). Website content was making me money (and I *enjoyed it). I decided to team up with web designers who didn't have writers on staff, so it would be a win-win scenario.*

2. Who are potential partners you can refer business to? What are their industries? (For example, financial advisors, realtors, others in your field with different ideal clients, and so on.)

EXERCISE 3: THE BRIGHT SIDE OF NETWORKING

It is always good business to connect two people even if you won't likely do business with either party. As you begin networking, you will likely run into people who aren't a match for your business but may be helpful to others. Begin tracking what industries those may be and how they may be good referrals for others in your network.

An easy way to begin cataloging this information is by writing a few quick notes on the back of the person's business card. Do it immediately after your meeting so the information is fresh. Note what you talked about and a few of your initial impressions so you can later follow up in an email. You can also use the chart below to help organize your thoughts and how this person may fit into your network

Contact	Industry	Their ideal client?	People I know that might be interested in this connection...
Example: Laura Smith	Promotional items such as water bottles, towels, keychains, etc.	Gyms, schools in the metro area	Kelly Johnson, VP of Marketing at the YMCA.

EXERCISE 4: THE DARKER SIDE OF NETWORKING

It's important to focus on what you *can* control when you find yourself in an uncomfortable networking situation. Dr. French recommends breathing first and foremost, which can both steady the neurochemicals in your brain and give you time to collect your thoughts. However, this takes practice, especially before you find yourself in a triggering situation. Set a timer for five minutes and practice this simple breathing exercise as often as you can, so you can return to it when you find yourself in a difficult position.

1. First, take one or two deep breaths, where your belly rises with a deep inhale and sinks with a deep exhale.
2. Continue this pattern, breathing in for a count of four.
3. Hold your breath for a count of four.
4. Exhale your breath slowly for a count of four.
5. Pause here, then repeat.

After you complete five minutes of this meditation, notice how you feel. What do you feel physically? Are your shoulders more relaxed? What you do feel emotionally? Do you feel calmer?

7

Set Your Boundaries

A bout eight months into starting my business, I experienced one of the worst interactions I've ever had with a client.

For the past three months, I had been working with this client on her logo and website. Designing logos was the rocky start to my business. I didn't especially enjoy it, but my clients were usually happy with what they got in the end. And this client was happy – until she wasn't.

Something had changed in the months since she had first become my client. What had started out as a positive connection with both of us excited to begin working together had turned into something else entirely. She started to ask for a lot of changes, which meant that the cost was beginning to escalate on the project. These changes required me to contract out some of the work to other vendors, and I wouldn't have the money to pay them if she didn't pay me more. So, I had to ask her to pay more. Because I had been running my business for only eight months, I was still too inexperienced to explain all of this to her in a way that wouldn't upset her. Instead, I flat-out explained: If you ask for more things, you have to pay for those additional things. This, unsurprisingly, didn't sit well with her. For her, it triggered the feeling of being taken advantage of, and, I suspect, the feeling that I was being ageist toward her. Additionally, the increase in cost bothered her, though she didn't say that outright. All her emotions – especially anger – rose to the surface when she said the following to me on a video call:

"Who do you think you are? I have a Ph.D. I'm not an idiot."
"You are ridiculous if you think I am going to pay this."
"I don't appreciate you speaking down to me."

Even though I was prepared for her not to want to pay more money, I was not prepared for her strong emotional response. I completely froze. I didn't know how to respond to her emotions. I tried to keep it professional. "If we add this..." I said, in an attempt to bring the conversation back to our work together, "then we need to account for that cost." But I only seemed to be doing more damage.

Eventually, I apologized, over and over. As soon as the call ended, I burst out crying.

All of us, at one time or another, have cried at work. Whether we did it in the privacy of our own office or quickly darted into a bathroom stall, we've all been there. And when you're working for yourself, that's not going to change. If anything, it will be amplified. That's because every element of your business that you have cultivated and grown is also a part of yourself that you have cultivated and grown. When someone calls you names, or refuses to pay you, it's nearly impossible not to take that personally. You aren't running a faceless organization like Bank of America or Delta Airlines. You're running a small business, where you're face to face with every client.

When I found myself crying at my desk after this terrible conversation, it was around three in the afternoon. Which meant that I still had work left to do. But I couldn't focus after what had happened. So, instead, I called my mom – my sounding board – and cried again.

I've told you this story so the same doesn't happen to you. Take it as a cautionary tale about what can happen when you're a business owner who hasn't set their boundaries. This client had crossed a line, in large part because I didn't have the right boundaries set up that would have slowed her to a stop. I should have ended the emotionally charged exchange or re-directed the conversation to a more productive space. Instead, I did not keep a strict boundary between us as business partners and allowed her to speak freely with me before this interaction. Without that boundary, she became accustomed to speaking to me as a friend. The result? Our professional business relationship was nonexistent and, therefore, normal business asks were unproductive.

Boundaries are incredibly important. Especially when you're first starting out in the business world, when you'll be working long hours and feeling anxious a lot of the time, you need to create boundaries. Even if doing so feels counterintuitive to getting as many clients as you can. Trust me: You can still do this and create a successful business.

I get it. You feel like you always need to be "on call" for client emergencies. Or like you should be available to answer potential clients' texts at nine o'clock at night, because the last thing you want to do is miss out on new business opportunities. I was the same way when I started my business. I had zero boundaries because I felt like I couldn't afford to have any. What happened? A client ended up texting me during my deep stretch yoga class at 8 p.m. on a Friday night, telling me that they had a "great idea" for their next marketing campaign and wanted to know my thoughts. Not only was I unable to fully unwind from my own day, but I also wasn't in a good mindset to respond to that client when, for me, I was off the clock. The fact is, I did not want to (nor did I need to) be making strategic marketing decisions on a Friday night. Whether I was at a relaxing yoga class or drinking a glass of wine to wind down, this time was for me, not for anyone else.

I still cringe when I think about how often I sacrificed personal time or even a vacation because I was too afraid to say no to a potential prospect in the hopes that they would turn into a long-term client. When you're in your first year in business, you can't help but think that any potential lead is a potential client. I often thought to myself, *If I go the extra mile for this prospect, they're going to want to work with me.*

Turns out this wasn't always the case. In fact, I found that people do not often notice you are going the extra mile, especially when you first begin working with them. This makes sense, though, right? They don't have a yard stick to measure what you "normally" do for clients, so if you are going above and beyond, using your personal time to help them with a project, they will likely think this is simply how you are, all the time. Therefore, they'll expect that from you, every time. I wish I had realized this much earlier in my business. Once I realized how much easier it made my life to A) set boundaries and B) stick to them, the more respectful and smoother my relationships with my clients became.

When a prospect or client knows that you're available during your personal time, or that you'll work while you're on vacation (even though they've seen your out-of-office email), they are not going to respect your boundaries because *you* don't respect your boundaries. I'm speaking from experience.

However, this isn't just beneficial for you, it's beneficial for your clients as well. Once I set my boundaries and worked according to them, I found that the quality of my clients increased greatly. I was calmer and happier, and, honestly, so were my clients. They knew when I would be available to them, and this created a sense of normalcy in our partnership. Previously, when our relationship had the expectation of "I'm here for you 24/7" despite the low fee they were paying me, clients expected that continuous level of interaction – without paying me any more money. By setting the boundary of: "This is when I'm available for us to talk," and including "additional costs" when a client wanted *another* meeting with me, the right clients happily paid it without problem, or backed off on their requests.

It will make the same difference for you.

In this chapter, you'll learn everything you need related to boundaries. In the first three sections, we'll review this information in the form of stories, so you can recognize boundary-crossing when it happens. In the last two sections, we'll go over boundary-setting strategies you can implement in the way you run your business. These sections run as follows:

1. Know Your Worth (Or Take a Loss Like a Boss)
2. Time is Money
3. Firing Toxic Clients
4. Boundaries 101
5. Red Flags and Saying No

KNOW YOUR WORTH (OR TAKE A LOSS LIKE A BOSS)

As you can imagine, I had to take on work I didn't love when I was first growing my business. (*Hello*, logo design.) Unfortunately, being hungry for work also meant that I made bad decisions. Specifically, I let people walk all over me, and I also agreed to less money so I could make myself seem more attractive to potential clients.

Once, I had a client interested in my work who wanted to sign me on for a four-month contract. This would have been my longest client contract to date. Four whole months of steady money? Where do

I sign? As we were discussing, I was asked to cut my rate (red flag number one) because it didn't fit into the client's budget (I've by now learned to ask about the client's budget before getting to this stage). So, I cut my hourly rate, then stood fast at that number. I knew how to create boundaries; I just wasn't putting them up soon enough.

Another problem that occurred with this client was that I began taking on a lot more work than I had budgeted time for. I tried to push back in some areas, but, at the end of the day, I needed the money. I caved. They needed me to complete X project, and, since they were a "long-term" client at that point, I thought, *Maybe this will show my dedication and it'll pay off in the long run.* Side note: Sometimes it will; sometimes it won't. Today, I am in a position financially and emotionally where I can call a timeout and say, "Sorry (not sorry), this isn't in our original agreement. If you'd like to add it, we can certainly discuss that." For the most part, it re-adjusts people. And for those that it doesn't, well, they can find another partner elsewhere. But I didn't have that luxury then – or didn't know I could have it.

What happened after two months of me trying to keep this client happy while I worked additional (non-paid) hours of work? I began to feel financially – and emotionally – stretched. So, I reconciled my calendar and my bank account.

To do this, I calculated exactly how much money I'd made during our time working together, and then I estimated the time I'd invested multiplied by my hourly rate of 100 dollars. I then determined how much money per hour I was actually making. I knew it would be lower. *As long as it isn't less than fifty dollars an hour,* I told myself,

I'll be okay. Instead, I was making less than twelve dollars an hour. I was working a full week, forty hours, maybe even more, and I was making about the same hourly rate as I had when I'd been a floral assistant at Kroger at sixteen years old.

I spoke to the client directly about the situation, first and foremost taking ownership of my role in the process. I then suggested how we could move forward in a way that would be beneficial for both of us. This included paying me going forward for the additional work I was currently providing. Of course, the client appreciated my hard work, but when we reviewed our agreement, they out-argued me on how I had defined my services. Unfortunately, with an industry like marketing, there's wiggle room in how services are defined. My client felt that I was still working within the boundaries of our agreement, even though I could list out another five to seven services I was currently providing that were not being covered financially.

I had two options after hanging up the phone. One, I could continue to go to battle over the additional hours that I wasn't being paid for, with the result of either finally arriving at an agreement with my client or completely destroying our relationship. Or, two, I could let it go.

Here's what happened first. I got angry. Really angry. Because of all the financial reasons above and also because of other reasons that had nothing to do with the situation at hand but that fed into my insecurity and into the feeling of being taken advantage of in this first year of business. The second thing that happened was that I called my dad, who has decades of experience with people. I asked him for his advice.

He told me to take the loss.

"It's not fair," he said, "but this is what happens in business." His reasoning? This was potentially a big client. They were going to bring me more work in the future. "Take the loss now, and you'll gain it back in the future," he said. "Plus, you have more knowledge now, so, going forward, you can create the language you need for your contracts – and stick to it – so your agreements cover any additional expenses in the future. This is a painful one, but it's a good lesson."

And that's exactly what happened. I was pretty sore about the situation for a few days, but I kept pushing on. Our original four-month contract ended, and although I was determined to never work with them again, they returned after a while with additional work. I calculated what I knew would be an expected amount of time for the work, *plus* created specific language in our new contract that covered me for any additional services which might become a part of our relationship.

I ended up moving forward with this client, which resulted in me making more than 20,000 dollars over the next several months. I enjoy doing the math, because it makes me feel better; that's a gain of over 17,000 dollars at the simple cost of swallowing my pride and taking the loss. If I had said, "I am never working with you again," which I had really wanted to, then I would have left a lot of money on the table.

I also learned a lesson about boundaries. I didn't stop the client from crossing my boundaries at the very beginning. First, they crossed a boundary on my cost. Second, they crossed a boundary on my time. Overall, they continued to cross a boundary on my *value*. From this situation, I learned how to *create* and *hold* my boundaries and make more money the second time around.

After that initial rough start, the client and I not only went on to have a financially beneficial relationship, but also a relationship with more clearly defined boundaries. Although it didn't happen overnight, the more I slung up arrows pointing to my boundaries and gently redirecting them, the better – and healthier – our relationship became. Eventually, there was no need to point to my boundaries as they became a natural, normal part of our relationship. The client stopped pushing back on my value. I felt heard and, just as importantly, I felt my time and value were respected.

TIME IS MONEY

I was very lucky (and worked very hard) to find the right contacts during my first few years in business. By the beginning of my second year, I had taken my foot off the gas of networking because I had made a contact who brought in a good amount of business for me. This client basically kept me afloat. I've heard from a lot of entrepreneurs that this can be common – you find that one "White Whale," and then you're able to sleep a little more soundly at night.

And I did.

Except for when I didn't.

Because large clients mean large problems. And large problems include texts in the middle of the night and opening your inbox to seventy-three emails. Yikes. This client was taking up way too much of my time. It was a problem.

It was sometime in the middle of my third year of business when I was complaining to my sales coach (again) about this specific client. I was unhappy. When they called, I felt a knot in my stomach. And, unfortunately, most of my income relied on them. So, my coach recommended that I begin to build an exit strategy, just as I had done when I was getting ready to leave corporate. It was the same process of asking myself the right questions and making the right calculations:

- ✓ How much is this client paying me? (Run a sales report from last year. We discussed the importance of running reports in Chapter 2.)
- ✓ What is that number divided by twelve? Let's say it's 3,500 dollars when you divide it by twelve.
- ✓ Which prospects do I have in the pipeline that are close to hiring me?
- ✓ Add the potential payment from those potential prospects together.
- ✓ Is the monthly income that would come from those prospects enough to reach that 3,500 dollars? Close.
- ✓ So, what other services do I need to sell to put me at that magic number every month, for the next six months? Easy. Either two social media packages or one content writing retainer.

Boom. Exit strategy planned.

I now had my eye on which prospects I needed to push to the finish line. I had come to terms with the fact I needed to replace my "White Whale" of a client because of their continuous disregard for my boundaries. I was in search of prospects who would not only financially fill the gap of losing this large client, but who would respect my boundaries. Furthermore, if I had another large client become a prospect, I knew how to strongly set my boundaries in place early on, so as not to repeat this situation. Setting boundaries isn't about keeping people out; it's about funneling the *right* people in.

FIRING TOXIC CLIENTS

When I first moved my business out of my small condo and into an official office space, I was beyond elated. I was also excited to create my Google Business page, list my official office address, and request reviews from happy clients. It felt like I had made it. I had space between work and home. I had a place to meet with clients so I wasn't constantly crisscrossing the city. It felt good in a lot of ways.

But then something happened that completely changed how good I was feeling.

I was working on a small writing project for a client. It was a tight turnaround, so I expected to work a little over the weekend to meet his deadline. I had the capacity: I had only promised one round of edits, so once he gave me his feedback, we would be able to tie a bow on the final project within a day or two.

Unfortunately, he was very unhappy with my work. Of course, this happens with subjective art forms like graphic design and writing. You can say, "That's good writing," or "That's a terrible logo," but someone else may not agree with you. For that very reason, I try not to knock anyone else's writing unless it's plagued with dozens of grammatical errors and reads as though it were processed by Google Translate. But when you have someone who disagrees with you about the quality of your work *and* has a God complex about their own abilities, you're in trouble. Because: *If you have the ability – like you say – then why did you hire me?*

This client was unhappy because he felt a specific topic should have been included in the article I was writing. We emailed back and forth, back and forth, for hours that Friday. I explained why that wouldn't work for his audience, but, when he insisted, I agreed to put it in. When I asked him for specific details on what points of that topic he wanted me to include, he became irate. *Shouldn't I know what he wanted to say in this article? How come I couldn't read his mind?* This wasn't about my writing. This was about him wanting to control a project that didn't need controlling. Carried away by his anger, he started scrambling for a valid reason to demand a refund (which he did) while verbally berating me. He called me a liar and said I had "tricked" him out of his money. I felt like saying, "Sir, if I was going to trick you out of your money, I would have tried for more than 250 dollars."

By Monday morning, he had left a nasty voicemail on my cell phone. At this time, I wasn't able to take his calls. I had other client priorities, and I had established the boundary that I was unavailable but would get back to him by that afternoon. His dozens of emails and numerous calls weren't going to move him up on my priority list.

That's when, by around noon on Monday, he left another voicemail threatening to come to my office so we could speak face to face. I was not, under any circumstances, okay with that. For some context, my office was just me. Once the door was shut, there was nowhere to go. Many women, and possibly some men, would feel very uncomfortable if a person who had verbally assaulted them all weekend was now making plans to visit their office space, where no one else would be around.

He might not have had any emotional, verbal, or physical boundaries, but I sure as hell did. I called him immediately and fired him on the spot. No, he would not get his refund, as I had tried to reasonably respond to his feedback. Without any constructive input from him, I said, I could not move forward with his project, and, based on his complete disregard of boundaries in a professional client relationship, we were not going to continue this conversation.

He wasn't happy. But he left me alone.

I sat in dread for days waiting for the one-star Google review to come trickling in. But at least I had stood up for myself and for my boundaries. In the beginning of my business, I might have worked longer to "fix" his problem. Not anymore. When someone pushes your boundaries, you feel it in your gut. And you know what you need to do. Point to the boundary line. Or turn them away all together. That's what I learned to do from this experience. Sometimes, when your boundaries aren't enough, you can use the biggest boundary: "No."

BOUNDARIES 101

About ten months into running my business, I was traveling to Richmond, Virginia, for a long weekend. On the drive Friday afternoon, I saw that I had a missed call from a prospect I had been chasing down. Her voicemail said she needed help with an advertising graphic. I thought, *Sure, I have my laptop with me. This sounds pretty simple, and I can get my graphic designer to start working on it first thing Monday.*

I called her back. Mistake Number One.

She explained her project, and I said, "Sounds simple enough!" Mistake Number Two. I didn't tell her it would need to wait until I was back in the office. Mistake Number Three. I told her to send me the project so I could take a look and get her a quote by that afternoon. Mistakes Numbers Four through Eighty-Seven.

I ended up spending pockets of the rest of that afternoon responding to her emails and finally nailing down the budget. Once she paid the invoice, I felt pretty good. It was 600 dollars, significant for a three-day project. But here's the thing. Once a client pays you, they think they own you. Especially when you have disregarded your own boundaries from the beginning.

After her credit card payment went through, I was toggling emails in between museum exhibit visits and having to step outside a loud restaurant when her calls came through. I didn't establish the boundary that I was on vacation even though we both knew I was, so she didn't have a boundary to respect. There was no one for me to be mad at except myself.

So that you don't have to learn the lesson of setting your own boundaries the way I did, I'll share some boundary-setting strategies with you. These include:

1. Being strict about when you're available
2. Charging for your time at the right rate
3. Giving yourself a break when you're away and at home
4. Knowing how to keep toxic people from unsettling you

Being Strict About When You're Available

As entrepreneurs, we are forced to confront what the balance between our work life and personal life looks like and how it can be maintained successfully for our own sake as well as for the sake of our business. In the first few weeks of running my business, I learned quickly that I needed to create a structured boundaries system not only for myself, but also for my clients, so that they would know what to expect from me and how our relationship would best work. That system evolved as the months went on, so I had many opportunities to establish my boundaries with clients as they evolved.

Eventually, my contracts even had a "Communications" clause

which established the times I was available (9 a.m. – 6 p.m., Monday through Friday). Perhaps some entrepreneurs might tell you that it's imperative that you be available 24/7. At least, that's what they told me. However, for my own health, and the health of my client relationships, I needed boundaries. It's important to have those boundaries listed as "white space" on your calendar, no matter your business or industry.

Here are some strategies you can use to be strict about when you're available:

1. **Stick to Your Office Hours:** By this I mean, stick to your office hours so it *seems* like you're doing it to the outside world. If you need to use the evenings/weekends to catch up with emails, I totally get it. Fortunately, with most email programs, you can schedule a send so that the client does not receive your email until 8 a.m. Monday. Do the work when you need to, but by all outward appearances, look like you're working normal business hours. That way, clients and other contacts will only expect you to be available during your office hours.

2. **Block out your calendar for administrative work:** I'm not a morning person, so I block out the first hour of my calendar every weekday to respond to emails and check my clients' social media feeds. Whenever someone asks me for a meeting, I never tell them I'm available before 10 a.m., even if I technically am, because that time is blocked out for administrative tasks.

3. **Keep your "out-of-office" message on,** all the time: I'm stealing this one from a client. He kept an out-of-office response up all the time, with a note that he was only checking his email during certain hours of the day. This wasn't necessarily true, he admitted, but it kept people in check for when they could expect to hear back from him. If they had "missed" that window when he was checking emails for the day, they knew he'd likely get back to them the next day.

Charging for Your Time at the Right Rate

I once heard from a fellow entrepreneur that she had a base rate with clients if she was thinking about them in the shower. Meaning: If she was thinking about her client's business strategy during a personal time (like showering), then they needed to pay her a specific base rate each month. Completely fair.

In fact, I have a hard and fast rule, and I'm not joking about this. If you want me to think about your business 24/7, the going rate *begins* at 25,000 dollars a month. That's how important my time is to me. Do I think about my clients off the clock? All the time. Do I sometimes respond to emails on weekends? You bet. Am I charging them 25,000 dollars a month? No... But the point is, I'm under no obligation to respond to them or think about them when I'm off the clock. I do it, not because they're paying clients, but because I enjoy my work. And if I'm taking a few days off for a vacation or enjoying my weekend, I don't feel like I have to apologize or explain myself. When clients behave as though their 175-dollar project warrants bothering me on the weekend, they're going to learn very quickly that I am not the right marketer for them.

In the first year of my business, would-be clients would sometimes haggle on price. It happens much less frequently now, but it can occasionally still become an issue. Early on, I remember a man saying to me, after receiving my proposal for my work, "You know I can hire my daughter's roommate at NC State to do this at a third of the cost." I paused. *Is he serious? How old/inexperienced does he think I am that my rate is comparable to that of a college student?* At the time, I didn't have the experience to navigate this type of comment, so I responded with, "Well, that's nice." Not strategic. Not helpful. And, in case you were wondering, no, I didn't close the sale.

Your time – like mine – is worth something. And it's important to be strict about the hours you are working for your clients so they know that your rate/cost is a guarantee of the time you're spending on their work. For example, when working in a regular corporate job, you are expected to be at your desk, completing work, by a certain time in the morning, and it's reasonable that you will leave by a certain time in the evening. You are being paid for those hours. The same is true when you're an entrepreneur; the only difference is that you are setting the rules for the hours you are paid, and how much.

When a client – or partner – begins to haggle on price in the beginning, you can expect with almost 100 per cent certainty that they don't see your value. Here are some strategies you can use for setting boundaries with clients and how to charge for your time at the right rate.

"Your Rate is Too High" (but the Client is Wrong)

When a client either haggles with you on price or flat-out says your cost is too high, there are two questions you can ask to re-direct the conversation and determine what your next step should be. You can either ask them:

1. "Have you worked with others in my industry before?" Or, if you already know the answer to this question is "yes," you can ask:
2. "What budget did you have set aside for this service/product?"

With the first question, there are two answers the client can give you. Often, they have not worked with someone in your space, therefore, they do not have a realistic idea of what the cost should be. Invite them to look at your competitors (you can do this because you've done the hard work of researching what a fair rate should be), and recommend they circle back after they've had time to research other options.

Otherwise, they may answer that they have worked with someone in your space but they cost less. If this is their response, push back for more details by asking, "And why are you not working with them again?" Chances are, they were unhappy with the quality of service, or there was another deciding factor not related to cost that caused them to begin a conversation with you. Either way, this should bring you back around to restating your original cost and the value you bring to the client.

Now, if a client has worked with others in your industry, but there are valid reasons why they aren't working with their previous vendor again (for example, that vendor no longer provides the service or product), then it's time for you to brainstorm with the client how you can cut down the price. When you ask them what their budget is, you will have a clear idea of what you *can* provide for them. No, you're not going to discount your prices, but you can cut some of your services so that your cost falls in line with what they are wanting to spend.

Finally, if they don't know their budget *and* they haven't worked with someone in your industry before, then you are speaking with a client who is likely not ready to make a purchase. That being said, encourage them to research others in your industry, or even recommend they look at hiring an intern or someone who wouldn't cost a lot of money and needs some experience. In this subtle way, you're reminding them that you are professional business and you charge professional business prices.

"Your Rate is Too High" (but *You're* in the Wrong)

Sometimes, it's not the client's fault that they expect different rates, but your own. You may be subconsciously putting out the message that you're worth less than your rates. If you're afraid you might be doing this, look at your own marketing and service offering and determine where there might be a disconnect.

Ask yourself:
- ✓ Why doesn't this person see my value?
- ✓ Do I need to change my core message?
- ✓ Do I need to educate my network better?
- ✓ Is this person truly looking to take advantage?

Where you can, and if needed, adjust your marketing. Change your messaging, graphics, or even the way you type your emails. It may be something as simple as taking out certain language that is causing your clients to think you are not worth your price. Furthermore, never hesitate to be clear and direct on the *value* you bring to clients. Tell them how you will alleviate their pain.

Giving Yourself a Break When You're Away and at Home

It wasn't until year two, when I took a vacation to Scotland, that I literally couldn't be available at all for the first time since starting my business. (The internet is spotty in the Highlands.) I'd prepared myself for this situation. In fact, what should have caused me great anxiety was actually one of the already numerous selling points of the trip. Of course, I could have paid for the international coverage, but that was an extra step I'd have to take to ensure that I stayed connected to work. With so much planning and packing to do for the trip already, I wasn't motivated to add that to my to-do list.

While on this trip, did I begin to have a nagging sensation in my brain, reminding me I needed to check my email? Did this cause me great withdrawal symptoms like any addict who is denied their source? Sure did. I felt angsty, and I was a little too assertive about checking my email and/or social media when I did run into pockets of Wi-Fi. I was glad, however, when being online wasn't an option for me, especially when first waking up or right before falling asleep. I had to actually read a book or put on the news if I wanted to distract myself. Work had to wait. It was siloed in a separate part of my brain for the better half of a week. Not quite long enough to break the habit of *wanting* to check in daily, but long enough to feel a great lift of responsibility.

When I returned from Scotland, I commented to a friend how wonderful it had felt to be disconnected. She asked me why I couldn't do that now. "Just turn on your airplane mode," she suggested. "No one can reach you then."

This made me think of the importance of giving yourself a break, even when you're running your own business. This is another important way of setting boundaries. Here are a few strategies to give yourself a break no matter where you are:

1. Set your phone to "airplane mode" and other similar options
2. Give yourself ground rules for when you're on vacation
3. Schedule limited times to check in with work
4. Make the most of your vacation with photos and videos

Set Your Phone to "Airplane Mode" and Other Similar Options

You can always set your phone to airplane mode to give yourself a break no matter where you are. However, there are baby steps you can take if you aren't ready to take this leap on a regular basis. You can schedule "blackout periods" where your phone is turned off, or you can put it on "silent" while you do something self-soothing. You can also schedule your phone to switch over to *Do Not Disturb* and only allow certain phone calls to come through after a specific time.

Finally, this is a simple, but very useful option – you can change your notification settings. What are you most bombarded with while you are networking or at events? Emails? Social media notifications? Cut through the noise and prioritize only the notifications that are *most* important to you during your working hours. For me, those are work emails and calendar notifications. I do social media work for my clients, but I do not take on any of the notifications for their accounts (I would lose my damn mind). Instead, I have a scheduled time every day when I check in on my clients' social media accounts. I don't even let my own social media notifications (personal or business) come through.

You can also put into place the awesomely bold boundary that was artfully executed by a graphic designer who took her vacations with her husband – hiking and kayaking around the country – very seriously. She had her regular cell phone, an iPhone, that was for personal use. And a gray Nokia, a heavy but compact brick, that she used as her business phone. She turned it on during business hours and turned it off when business was done. Clients did not have her personal number, and if she was traveling, the gray Nokia wouldn't travel with her.

Give Yourself Ground Rules for When You're on Vacation

It also helps to create some ground rules for yourself when you're on vacation. These are mine, which I created so that I can enjoy my trips without simultaneously running my growing business into the ground. Feel free to model yours on mine or to change them as needed.

1. Take the laptop, but only use it while sitting in airports/on planes.

2. Don't respond to every email. Let your out-of-office response handle it.

3. Prep your clients before you leave and set realistic expectations. "I won't be responding to email, but do call me if there is an emergency. Also, this is what constitutes an emergency..."

4. Check in with clients before you leave and upon your return – even if you haven't heard from them. Let them know they're still at the top of your priority list.

5. Give yourself a generous runway both before you leave and when you return. Push any meetings and one-on-ones back so you show up fresh and well-rested – not cranky and tired.

Schedule Limited Times to Check in with Work

A friend of mine is fair-skinned, and when she took a family vacation to the beach, she decided to use the hottest hours of the day as her "vacation break," during which she would check in on work. She didn't want to get sunburned anyway, so it was a natural time for her to take solace inside. She used these couple of hours to check in on work and handle any projects she needed to. Consider where in your vacation schedule you can check in on work (only if you really want to), but with a limited time frame so that you aren't working a full day when you should be enjoying your vacation.

Make the Most of Your Vacation with Photos and Videos

This is one strategy that helps me enjoy my surroundings while providing future content for my marketing. For example, I love coming across old advertisements from the '50s and '60s that are marketed toward women (or are about women's roles), because they're fascinating (and funny) to me. When I come across any of this content, I usually snap a photo with a future social media post in mind for when I return to the office. The content of vintage marketing for women is both entertaining for my audience *and* on brand for my business.

How to Keep Toxic People from Unsettling You

Entrepreneurship is the Wild West. There are no rules or human resource departments, so when someone acts like a jerk, we have to figure out a way not to let it get to the core of who we are. Rather, we have to learn how to move forward as gracefully as we can. Sitting and stewing and wanting to punch that person in the face I totally get, but all of that energy needs to be focused on the good you are doing. The good that is your business and your goals. And, guess what? You don't have to work with those people. If someone doesn't align with your values or beliefs, or, worse, treats you in any manner that makes you uncomfortable, it is your prerogative to say, "No, thank you. I will find business elsewhere."

Here are some strategies you can use to keep toxic people from unsettling you, provided by Dr. French:

✓ Breathe.

✓ Establish a daily practice that allows you to cultivate presence with yourself. Meditation is a great way to do this.

✓ Honor your boundaries.

✓ When you notice your energy is drained by someone, take a break.

✓ Take time to notice the people and projects that *give* you energy.

✓ When at all possible, prioritize the people and projects that fuel you/energize you!

RED FLAGS AND SAYING NO

Maybe you're good at giving all your time away, and you thrive on being in touch with your clients all the time. Congrats, *and* I hope you are charging people for that time. That said, there are some behaviors you should definitely watch out for, even if you tend to bend over backward for your clients. It's very important to know what these red flags are, so that you can identify people who won't respect your boundaries.

In my experience, people who don't respect your boundaries will:

- Always expect something for free (or haggle with you incessantly on cost)
- Be late in getting back to you about deadlines
- Be late in paying you
- Take a long time making decisions
- Not know their budget for your services
- Often remind you that they have a family member or a close friend who is also in your industry, which is a sign that they consider themselves expert-adjacent and will question many of your decisions

As an entrepreneur, you'll find that some people handle the stress of a project or business relationship better than others. For me, as someone who tries to manage stress as best I can, it has become increasingly difficult to work with people who don't. If you're sitting on a phone call with a client, and you aren't sure if you're going to get Dr. Jekyll or Mr. Hyde when you deliver news, it's not a healthy relationship. Even if they are paying you good money, it's downright exhausting. I had a client that, at first, was a great client, but then they started paying me late, and then giving me the impression that they were annoyed about me asking for the money. Finally, they started losing their cool about almost any tiny thing. It affected my overall health and made me re-evaluate whether it was worth continuing to work with them. I decided that it wasn't, and after I informed them that our professional relationship would come to an end, I felt a great weight had been lifted. Because they were hard to please (like many toxic clients are), they were just as happy about the parting as

I was, and they were ready to move on to another business, hoping it would be a much more successful relationship. After ending that connection, I found that I had more energy and patience with my other clients, not to mention I was sleeping better at night.

People want to work with people who give them good energy and good vibes, even if they don't realize it. If you aren't taking care of yourself, you won't give off good vibes, and if you aren't giving off good vibes, no one will want to work with you. So, save your energy for people who are good to work with. Say no to the wrong people and yes to the right ones. People who respect your boundaries respect you, which means that they're going to be open to collaboration and conversation, and they're not going to easily leave you. And they are (this is a big one) going to pay you what you are worth.

A Note on Women and Boundaries

I feel that women have a hard time with boundaries, and that we all need extra support in saying no.

You may have heard this before, but the first time I heard it, it was life-changing. I was having coffee with a small group of women, sitting around another wooden table in another bustling coffee shop. One woman was struggling with the boundaries between her profession and her homelife. A mother to a toddler, she was strapped for time and valued creating those boundaries. She just had a hard time doing so. Another, older (read: wiser) woman across the table said to her:

"No is a complete sentence."

As women, we forget this all the time. We struggle to say no. And when we do say no, we always feel we have to apologize or explain why we can't do something. Then, we overexert ourselves later to make up for it, or beat ourselves up over our decision. However, by saying no, not only are you making a healthy choice for you and your business, but you're also creating a healthy option for *all* women. When we see our peers say no with confidence, it normalizes boundaries for all of us.

So, when you want to say no to a project or a person, you can, and absolutely need, to do it. If it's a complicated relationship, such as one with a client, you are going to need to use some blanket statements such as: "It's not a good fit," or "That goes beyond our scope." I know. This can be uncomfortable. And, spoiler alert: Half the time, you're going to have to say "no" to some really nice people.

Men have an easier time with saying no, and also with maintaining their boundaries. They're certainly less likely to apologize for their boundaries. When I created my working hours of 9 a.m. to 6 p.m., I found myself having to explain to people why I didn't want that 8 a.m. call. "I'm not in the office by then," I would say (true), or I'd say, "You're just not going to get me at my best that early in the morning," (more true).

For some reason, I was having a hard time believing that people would accept my boundaries. This might be a gender issue. Now, I know plenty of men (and I'm related to one of them), who fill every waking hour of the day with work and/or thinking about work. But men who do set boundaries have never felt the need to apologize to me. "When you own your business, why should you have to get up early?" one said to me. "I am not a morning person," he continued, sipping his coffee, "so I don't take a meeting before 9 a.m." He didn't have to justify it. He was the boss. And if he didn't want a meeting before 9 a.m., he wasn't going to have one. End of discussion.

Boundary-Making is a Practice

It takes practice to set your boundaries. To be honest, you probably won't be able to successfully do this on a regular basis for a while. It takes a lot of time to learn to say no to some things or to set your limits, especially when it feels like you can't say no to anything. But it's something to strive toward, even if you're only taking a fifteen-minute break in the beginning. When you know that you have a busy day packed with meetings/phone calls, consider padding your time in between your commitments to take a break. Again, this doesn't have to be an extended period of time. Set a timer if you need, but do something that will bring you joy. You could go for a quick walk, watch some funny videos on YouTube, read a chapter of a book, or listen to a podcast. Set those very simple boundaries at first, and notice how much better you feel once you return to the rest of your responsibilities with a clearer head. After that, try some bigger boundaries and *then* notice how great you feel. I promise it will become addictive, in the best possible way.

End-of-Chapter Check-In

EXERCISE 1: BOUNDARIES 101

It's easier to say no or to push back on clients when you have guidelines for what you will tolerate and what you will not. Here, we can practice what those boundaries may look like. Try brainstorming your answers to these questions:

1. I mentioned earlier that a client would have to pay me 25,000 dollars a month for me to be available to them 24/7. What is the amount of money you need to be paid to be available 24/7? What do you expect it to be once your business grows? (Note: "There is not enough money in this world," is also a correct answer.)

2. What are your business hours?

3. What is your preferred method for being in touch with clients? Phone? Text? Email? How will you "train" your clients to communicate with you this way?

4. How do you define a true "business emergency" in your industry? What is an example of that?

EXERCISE 2: RED FLAGS AND SAYING NO

In this chapter, I've outlined some general red flags that you will come across as a new entrepreneur. Regardless of your industry, there will likely be some general areas where clients will throw up a red flag. Start with asking yourself these questions as you get to know your clients better:

- Do they focus on price?
- Do they continuously talk about how well their business is doing? (From what you can tell, are they doing well?)
- How communicative are they when you ask a question?
- Have they worked with others in your industry before? Why did they quit working with them?

$$\left(\begin{array}{c}8\end{array}\right)$$

Face the Setbacks

Whatever setbacks you run into when you're starting out as an entrepreneur – whether it's a difficult day with a nasty client, or a month when you're worried about paying your bills – you need to face them. This will make you not only a better entrepreneur, but also a stronger person. In its own weird way, being an entrepreneur not only makes you good at running a business, but also makes you better at living your life.

In this chapter, we'll cover the different setbacks you'll face and how to deal with them. The different sections include:

1. Navigating calm seas and stormy skies
2. How to adapt and overcome
3. Failure
4. When to adjust your direction

NAVIGATING CALM SEAS AND STORMY SKIES

As I'm writing this book, I am beginning my third year in business. Yet, I'm constantly re-learning the same lessons I learned in my first year, just as I'm sure I will have to re-learn them again when I'm in year five, ten, and beyond.

Just a few months ago, I had a busy week full of proposals and meetings. I looked at my calendar and thought to myself, *By the end of this week, I'll either have three new clients or I'll be very depressed.* After preparing for each call, following up, and agreeing to terms, I did, in fact, sign three clients in five days. This was a result of months of hard work, and it was just a coincidence that all three were at the closing stage on the same week. Needless to say, I celebrated with the good Scotch that Friday evening.

Monday morning came, and I was still riding high from the wins of the prior week. However, by 11:30 a.m., I had lost a client. Not just any client, but my only retainer client, who was not only a big client financially, but also a great client operationally. They were my ideal client. I was heartbroken and, at first, a little nervous about what this meant for the business. But I reminded myself that this was why I needed to celebrate the wins, like I had the week before. Nothing is steady when you're an entrepreneur, even if you feel like it might be.

Everyone will tell you this. In your first year in business – and for many to come – you are going to have some really big highs, followed by some really big lows. Despite everyone telling new entrepreneurs this, I'd somehow believed that I was going to beat this struggle that all entrepreneurs face. Whenever I had one really good day (or a really good morning), I would be convinced that I had "made it," and that worrying about money or the next business opportunity would be in the past. I've learned that this is a natural feeling for most entrepreneurs. And that makes sense. After all, if you didn't believe that every high meant you had "made it," how would keep up the energy to keep going?

Shocker: After such a high, reality would usually smack me against the head a few hours later with another low.

You have to be prepared for those lows. And you will have to be patient. There is a lot of good work you need to do in your first year of business that will not yield results. You will need to meet *a lot* of people, you will need to market your business (cheaply), and you will need to reschedule your life so you don't lose your mind. There will be projects you don't like. There will be coffees that are a waste of time. There will be lean months and friends you rarely see, but hopefully you know by now that this is temporary. Going forward, yes, these moments will hit again – for days and weeks, but not for months on end (unless something has gone completely wrong). Your first year of business will be tough and dirty, so that the following years can be exactly what you had hoped they would be.

Are you going to be annoyed during that first year? You bet. Are you going to struggle financially? Most likely. Are you going to lose sleep and possibly do other unhealthy things? Some days more than others.

The good news? You'll get through it. It's all about using the right strategies. These include:

1. Celebrating your milestones
2. Embracing the highs and lows
3. Remembering that you have a support network
4. Reminding yourself why you chose the entrepreneur life

Celebrate Your Milestones

By the end of my first year, I began to learn exactly what was worth celebrating for me. At first, I celebrated the one-on-one meetings. Then, I celebrated being able to write a proposal for someone. Then, I celebrated them agreeing to the proposal and signing a contract. Eventually, I was at a place where I was celebrating new business regularly.

This first year will make or break you. Most people, if they find business ownership isn't the right fit for them, will go back to their previous jobs or previous industries. (There is *nothing* wrong with that. More on that later in this chapter.) Because of the challenges you'll face, you'll need to pep-talk yourself even more this first year than you thought. That's because you will be your worst critic. That said, take a moment to savor success when things go well, and, when things go not-so-well, remember the importance of the lessons you've learned.

Mark Your Calendar: 10 Milestones to Celebrate in Your First Year!

In October of 2017, before having quit my day job, I put on my favorite blue blazer and nude heels and drove the ten minutes into Uptown Charlotte to officially register my company name: Next Page Brand Strategies. As the woman was filing the paperwork, she asked me about my business. "We provide marketing for small businesses," I said cheerily, not entirely sure what I meant by that. "No way," she said, leaning over the counter. "I have a hair salon over on Tryon and *need* marketing help. Do you have a website?" As a matter of fact, I did. I wrote it down on the back of a receipt, and she gave me her business card. She did not become a client, but I walked out of that building feeling lighter than air. It was 8:45 a.m. on a Tuesday. As I drove into work to officially start my workday, I felt like I was already succeeding at owning this business stuff. *How hard could this really be?* I thought.

It was an incredible feeling, reaching those first milestones that day: registering my company name, meeting a potential client, exchanging contact details with her. They were worth celebrating and would help me stay motivated as I moved forward in my entrepreneurial journey. By doing the same for yourself, you'll get through the calm seas and stormy skies of being an entrepreneur.

Here are ten milestones worth celebrating:
1. Registering your company name
2. Receiving your first box of business cards
3. Launching your website
4. Attending your first networking event
5. Scheduling your first coffee/meeting
6. Sending your first proposal
7. Signing your first contract
8. Receiving your first payment!
9. Receiving a referral from a partner
10. Receiving an inquiry from your ideal client through your website (a cold lead)

At the End-of-Chapter Check-In, I've included a chart with additional space for you to capture other milestones as well. I encourage you to keep track of your milestones and celebrate every win – even small ones.

Embrace the Highs and Lows

Life is full of highs and lows. You don't have to be a business owner to experience that. However, it's easy to feel like you want to throw in the towel when you hit a low point in your entrepreneurial journey, because that's human nature. When things become difficult, we don't naturally want to embrace that low point and appreciate what it means.

And what does it mean? It means the highs are likely around the corner. That's true in business as well as life. You will have good days and bad days, and it's important to embrace both sides of this coin. Because without the highs *and* the lows, you won't grow your business (more on that later when we discuss failure).

Remember that You Have a Support Network

Back in Chapter 3, we covered the importance of creating a support network for yourself. When you're having a difficult time, you need to remember that you're not alone in this.

Even if friends and family don't always understand the struggles you face as a business leader, or sometimes say the wrong thing without intending to, you have people to turn to. You may be in front of a client or prospect by yourself, but there is always an army behind you.

When you reach out to your support network, you'll need to think about who's going to be most helpful to you in the context of the specific situation you're dealing with. This process is similar to how you reach out to certain friends for certain things when you're going through a breakup. You have the one friend who is going to be rational and help you move forward, and you have the other friend who will be quick – and happy – to list all the reasons your ex sucked. It should be the same for business. Do you need rational advice? Or do you need someone to bad-mouth that other person/situation even if they know nothing about that person/situation? Sometimes, you might need both. Whomever you end up choosing when reaching out to your support network, consider adding an important third contact: a trusted business partner. After you've reached out to people to support you personally and emotionally, consider what you can do to practically adjust to the problem you've encountered. Then, reach out to a trusted business partner who may be able to provide valuable feedback on your solution, or partner with you in making it a reality.

Remind Yourself Why You Chose the Entrepreneur Life

The truth is, I have no idea what hurdles you will come across in your business. In this book, I am speaking to the general growing pains of owning any business; all of us will have our own unique, painful stories to tell. But we will grow from them. So, the best advice I can give you for when those hurdles arise is to stand your ground. Dig your heels in. Make a pros and cons list if that helps. People will tell you (often) that starting a business is risky and scary, because it is. But you have your reasons for starting it, and no one can take those away from you, no matter how hard they try.

There will come a day when you ask yourself: *Why the hell am I doing this?* You may look to see if your job at your previous company has been filled. You may stare wide-eyed at your bank account and feel a knot in your stomach.

Here's what I recommend you do when that happens:

Write out five reasons why you left your old job. Add to this list now, and re-read it every time you feel your courage wane.
- Reason 1 I left that job:
- Reason 2 I left that job:
- Reason 3 I left that job:
- Reason 4 I left that job:
- Reason 5 I left that job:

Once you've written down your list of reasons why you left your previous job, make sure you keep it nearby, either pinned on your office wall or saved in an easy-to-access folder on your laptop. You should also take a look at this list here of the many positives of owning your own business. Let them be a reminder that you're doing all of this for really good reasons:

- ✓ Working in your pajamas (or at least pajama pants)
- ✓ Spending more time with your loved ones (furry or otherwise) at home
- ✓ Not being required to start your day at a specific time
- ✓ You're the boss!
- ✓ Not taking a phone call or meeting until 10 a.m. because you're not a morning person
- ✓ Not working past 4 p.m. because you *are* a morning person
- ✓ Choosing your signature clothing style
- ✓ Buying fun office/desk accessories that are stylish and functional

- ✓ Creating your own hashtag (and using it!)
- ✓ Exploring new coffee spots you never knew existed in your city
- ✓ Listing the new friends you have in your network

It also helps to remind yourself what you're grateful for. Not only as an entrepreneur, but as a person. Here's an example from my blog that helped me get through a hard day:

"Today, I am Grateful," posted on October 23rd, 2018

I'm going to be honest with you guys. Today has not been a good day. I sat down to write about what these "bad days" look like for an entrepreneur and "How to learn from them!" or some other convenient lesson like that. But instead, I'm choosing to be grateful for what this lifestyle has taught me and for what I have in this moment.

I am stressed. I have definitely cried today. I am exhausted. And I am grateful.

- ✓ *I am grateful that I have an amazing team of people who work with me through the creative process – and who are always on my side to problem-solve and laugh (and sometimes drink) together.*

- ✓ *I am grateful for other marketing professionals who are ten, fifteen, and twenty years ahead of me in their careers, who have taken my calls or sat down with me for a cup of coffee just so I could pick their brain.*

✓ I am grateful for the clients that have become friends. Who have trusted me to become a part of their business and – by extension – part of their family.

✓ I am grateful that I can say "no" to opportunities when my plate is too full.

✓ I am grateful for being in Charlotte. A city with a strong, warm, and welcoming entrepreneurial community.

✓ I am grateful for my friends (local and long-distance) who tell me how amazing I'm doing, even if they don't really know if I am or not.

✓ I am grateful for former co-workers, acquaintances, long-distance family, and old friends who follow my social media channels even if they will never need my services.

✓ I am grateful that my parents are the first people to tell me, "Don't quit. Keep going."

✓ I am grateful for my sister, who can help me normalize what is annoying (or actually not working) with social media when my patience is gone, and who has offered to help me manage my own channels on the days they fall to the back burner.

✓ I am grateful for Max, who does not let me sit at my computer past 6 p.m. when I should be feeding him dinner, and who *reminds me that a walk in the middle of the afternoon is good for both of us.*

HOW TO ADAPT AND OVERCOME

Over the years of running my own business, I've had to adapt when necessary.

A recent example is how I had to change the way I did business during the pandemic in 2020. This time reminded me that there are often mornings, days, and weeks when, if I take my foot off the gas, my business could evaporate. As the world economy braced for shutdowns of industries across the globe, I continued to hustle. I called on the contacts in my pipeline. I warmed leads that had gone cold. I began creating free webinars for contacts to access. I remained top-of-mind and leaned into the values I believed would be the biggest source of support for other small businesses. I did not hide behind the shut-down or self-quarantine (well, not digitally). I may have been at home, working from the kitchen table, but I was working harder than ever.

It was during this time that I witnessed a great example of entrepreneurial pivoting. A friend of mine, an aesthetician who provided facials and other skin treatments in her space, was forced to shut her doors. At the beginning of the pandemic, it was unclear when the social-distancing rules would allow her to see clients again. She did not wait to see what the county or state would allow. Within weeks, she had launched a new beauty subscription box that included at-home skin treatments, a tailored Spotify station, herbal tea, and YouTube videos that would help her clients nourish their skin from the inside out. Her business was not defined by the pandemic; it evolved because of it. That's what entrepreneurs do. They adapt. They find a new way. They rise.

No matter what business you are in, and regardless of whether there's a global pandemic going on, something is going to fail, and that means that you need adapt and overcome.

Here are some strategies for how to adapt and overcome:

Expect the Best; Plan for the Worst

I know this is an old adage that may have lost its meaning with years of overuse, but it's really the best strategy to use when you begin your business. You're excited to start this new business; you are optimistic, full of energy, and, of course, you believe everything is going to be amazing and work out exactly how you had hoped. You wouldn't be doing this if you didn't feel that way.

However, it's important to have a backup plan for that one project or service. Maybe have a couple of backup plans. Especially if you're relying on a new business partner to support you on a project, have another phone number in your back pocket. When the world goes sideways on you, be sure to have another option. You need to create your own safety net.

Regular Check-Ups

For the life of your business, you will want to keep your finger on the pulse of the current economic and industry landscape. However, during your first year in business, you will likely be required to adapt and overcome more frequently as you work to establish yourself. For example, you may be providing a service that isn't bringing in money. When your business is young, you need to pivot much quicker to ensure you are moving closer to the *right* and profitable service that will sustain you.

Ask yourself: *Am I making money? Which service is my least profitable? Where can I cut costs?* There will always be outside forces that will affect the direction of your business and it's important to get comfortable asking yourself these important questions. Your ability to pivot and adjust every few months in your first year of business will help you overcome most hurdles you face in the long term.

FAILURE

This one is going to hurt. But you have to know this: Failure is okay – and necessary – when you're growing your business. Some entrepreneurs are more comfortable with this fact than others. Many successful entrepreneurs actually embrace it. That may sound crazy, but it will sound less crazy once you've read the following example.

You've probably heard of *The Huffington Post*. And you might know about the woman behind it: Ariana Huffington. Like many entrepreneurs who are now running a famous business, she had to deal with failure. In 2003, Ariana Huffington ran for Governor of California. Her run was a failure. "My mother used to call failure a stepping-stone to success, as opposed to the opposite of success," said Huffington. "When you frame failure that way, it changes dramatically what you're willing to do, how you're willing to invent, and the risks you'll take."[11]

Huffington learned a lot from her failed gubernatorial run. She learned many lessons about the power of the internet, communicating, and how to listen. These lessons had a great impact on the strategies she used to launch *The Huffington Post*. As of 2015, the digital media outlet was valued at one billion dollars.[12] Far from the opposite of success.

I don't have a one-billion-dollar company (yet). But I have failed. I have lost time. I have lost the equivalent of three months' pay. And those failures have been side-steps into success.

I get that failure is a scary thing. My biggest fear when I was starting my business was: *What if I fail?* I had enough savings to float me for three months, so if absolutely nothing came in, I still had a three-month safety net. Thankfully, I didn't need to start using it until Q3. That's also when I started to seriously consider going back to Corporate America. And yet, despite this three-month security net,

---

[11] Lapowsky, Issie. "Arianna Huffington: Dare to Fail." Inc.com, Inc., 24 Jan. 2013, www.inc.com/magazine/201302/rules-for-success/arianna-huffington-dare-to-fail.html.
[12] Somaiya, Ravi. "Huffington Post in Limbo at Verizon." *The New York Times*, The New York Times, 3 June 2015, www.nytimes.com/2015/06/03/business/media/huffington-post-in-limbo-at-verizon.html.

I was afraid of failure. It's totally normal and very common to feel this way, especially when you're first starting out, and it is the only way to move forward in entrepreneurship. Your failures become the building blocks for your business.

In my own life, learning *how to accept* failure is probably the greatest lesson I've learned. I learned this lesson even before starting my business, when I was going through my divorce. I had to learn to accept the "failure" of my marriage, which strengthened my ability to accept failure generally.

It's also a very humbling experience when you are going through a difficult period in your life and look up, covered in sweat and blood, and hear unwelcome commentary from people sitting in the cheap seats. They, unscathed, because they haven't taken big risks in life, will provide feedback based on nothing but their own opinion. With my divorce, any decision on romantic relationships after that were, for some reason, up for debate. The same thing happened with my business. Those who were not true friends and family had critical feedback on my life choices. They quickly fell out of the orbit of my inner circle.

Brené Brown captures this much more eloquently in her book *Rising Strong.* In the introduction, she explains the famous quote from Theodore Roosevelt's "Man in the Arena" speech in 1910, which became the epitaph for her important research on vulnerability:

> "It's not the critic who counts; not the man who points out how the strong man stumbles or where the doer of deeds could have done them better. The credit belongs to the person

who is actually in the arena, whose face is marred with dust and sweat and blood; who strives valiantly... who at the best knows in the end the triumph of high achievement, and who at the worst, if he fails, at least fails while daring greatly."

Brown goes on to say that these "facedown" moments can be big (like getting fired or getting a divorce) or they can be small (like struggling with a child who's lied about a report card or experiencing a disappointment at work), but *we* become the writers of how those disappointments, or perceived failures, shape us. She writes, "When we own our stories, we avoid being trapped as characters in stories someone else is telling."[13]

At the end of the day, the ability to accept failure as an important part of success, coupled with the strength to tell my own story, helped me build the grit needed for owning a business. But, don't worry, *you* don't have to get a divorce to learn how to accept failure. It's simply a matter of learning how to be grateful for opportunities even when they don't work out the way we want. If you can't find the positives in failing, owning a business is going to be really hard.

You'll fail in small ways and in big ways. You'll make mistakes that cost you thousands of dollars – and trust me when I say it's not easy to look at one of those mistakes and say, "Well, let me figure out how not to do that again..." However, if you begin with gratitude for the opportunity to learn and move forward, you're well on your way to success.

---

[13] Brown, Brené. "Truth and Dare." *Rising Strong*, Random House USA, 2017, pp. xviii-xix.

Failure Isn't an Option; It's a Guarantee

Accepting failure isn't going to happen overnight. But failure *is* going to happen. So, it's important to learn how to deal with it in a positive way. It takes practice, like anything else you'll be doing in your first years of business and beyond. As you begin that practice, here are some helpful strategies:

- Normalize failure. Turn to books, documentaries, or TedTalks about others who have failed. You're in good company.

- Find comfort. Whether it's eating a specific food, making an expensive purchase, or simply an afternoon of sitting on the couch under a weighted blanket and re-watching Seasons 1 and 2 of *Fleabag*, do it. Whatever brings you comfort, let yourself indulge in it for an afternoon or evening.

- Make a list. You will have learned something from this failure. What is it? What will you not do again in the future? What will you adjust? Make this failure count so it increases your chances of success in the future.

What Happens If My Business Fails?

Alright. Here it is. Perhaps your biggest fear of starting a business.

What happens if you aren't able to make this new lifestyle work? What happens if you decide, in your first year of business, that you can't take the stress, either financially or emotionally, or that it just isn't what you thought it would be? What happens if you "fail" at owning a business and go back to your previous job or previous industry?

Nothing happens.

You'll continue breathing. The birds will keep chirping. The sun will rise in the east tomorrow.

Here's the thing: Changing direction is not a failure. You can't really fail at owning a business. You own one or you don't. And when you don't, people don't categorize you as a failure.

The fact is, nothing is guaranteed. In life. In love. In business. What is working today may not work tomorrow. That's the thing about all of this. Even if we can't predict what's on the next page, we know, deep in our soul, that the story is still worth writing.

WHEN TO ADJUST YOUR DIRECTION

When I began my business, I knew what I wanted to do and what I didn't want to do. I also knew that there were some projects (okay, a lot of projects) that I needed to do because I had to eat. In that first year, my business was not quite where I wanted it to be, but after a few disastrous detours (looking at *you*, logo design), I was beginning to learn what direction I needed to take.

Here is what I wanted:
- ✓ To develop the big-picture marketing strategy of businesses
- ✓ To work with established (ten-plus years) businesses

Here is what I did not want:
- ✓ To develop social media
- ✓ To work with non-profits

By the end of my first year:
- ✓ I was focused on social media
- ✓ My biggest client was a non-profit

Clearly, something had to change.

So, at the end of my first year, I consciously moved away from non-profit work. Look, I love working with non-profits, because they all have such great missions. Who doesn't want to work with a non-profit? The problem, though, is that working with a non-profit is pretty much pro-bono work, and this wasn't a solid business plan for my goals. So, I pivoted and raised my prices.

I also needed to accept the fact that people were looking at me as a social media guru when I didn't believe myself to be one. I was getting a lot of social media work because a lot of people didn't want to do it. But I found that, by securing my niche so that I was doing the kind of social media work I enjoyed (writing and big-picture strategy), I could find a complement between what I wanted to do and the needs of the marketplace. I was inching closer to a sustainable business.

The fact is, adjusting your direction by changing your business goals over time is a big part of running your business. The focus is to keep moving your business moving forward purposefully. Here are some best practices for resetting your business goals and moving forward so that you can adjust your direction:

- **Talk to the people:** I love a good questionnaire. Reach out to people in your network who are your ideal client and who you have an established, friendly relationship with. Ask their opinion on the services you are currently offering and what services they would perhaps like to see. You might be surprised by what you hear.

- **Acknowledge your weak spots:** If you're not great at self-reflection in this area (and few of us are), turn to a trusted mentor or friend. What can you strengthen either personally or professionally? Armed with this information, consider attending webinars in the areas you want to improve or partnering with another business to enhance your service offering for certain clients.

- **Take action:** One of the biggest mistakes you can make as an entrepreneur is inaction. You need to do something. Even if you're not sure it's the *right* next step (and it might not be), look at the information you have available and move forward.

For example, did your ideal client mention a service in your industry that they need? If you have the skillset, or the right project partner, try it. If it works, great. If it doesn't work, you will have new information on where to re-direct yourself next. Win-win.

End-of-Chapter Check-In

EXERCISE 1: NAVIGATING CALM SEAS AND STORMY SKIES

It's important to celebrate your major milestones the first year you are in business and to keep that list handy, especially when you have tougher days. Use the chart below to keep track of your progress. After you've reached all of these milestones, begin adding your own.

Milestone	Date Achieved!	Celebration Plans
Registering your company name		
Receiving your first box of business cards		
Launching your website		
Attending your first networking event		

Milestone	Date Achieved!	Celebration Plans
Scheduling your first coffee/ meeting		
Sending your first proposal		
Signing your first contract		
Receiving your first payment!		
Receiving a referral from a partner		
Receiving an inquiry from your ideal client through your website (a cold lead)		

EXERCISE 2: HOW TO ADAPT AND OVERCOME

Unfortunately, you won't be able to predict when it'll be necessary to adapt and overcome. Just know that once you recognize a part of your business isn't working, you'll want to take action quickly. Use these questions to help prepare yourself:

1. What's the problem? (Low funds, chaotic scheduling, unhappy clients, etc.)
2. What process can you stop immediately?
3. What process do you need to keep but reassess?

EXERCISE 3: FAILURE

Remember: The most successful people you know have failed. You will fail, too. It might hurt, but it's a very important step to owning a business.

1. Google five people whom you admire in business.
2. Of those five, how many of them have failed, and what have they said about their failure?
3. In your life, prior to now, how have you failed before? A test? A soccer game? An important relationship? Another personal goal?
4. And you're still standing. What did that failure teach you about the next one you have yet to encounter?

EXERCISE 4: WHEN TO ADJUST YOUR DIRECTION

When it's time for you to adjust direction, you may be making an internal change (for example, how you define your ideal client), an external change (for example, how you market to your ideal client), or a combination of both. Use this flowchart to determine the direction you need to move in. I have provided an example to help.

Current Hurdle	→	What's the problem?	→	Where do I want to be?	→	What can I change immediately?	→	What requires more planning?
Low sales	→	My ideal client isn't buying my services	→	I need more sales.	→	I can create a new Client Avatar	→	I need to restructure my packages and adjust my core message for ongoing marketing

Then, list your next steps and to-do items to put this change into action immediately.

Conclusion:
This is Your Story

When I began my entrepreneurial journey, I had more nay-sayers than cheerleaders. Mostly, I felt that they didn't understand why I was taking the unnecessary risk. They wouldn't ask outright, but I knew what they were thinking:

Why leave a comfortable, salaried job for a financial unknown?

You're very shy around people you don't know, so how do you plan to network and sell?

Girl, you did not go to business school. How do you think you're qualified to do this?

Honestly, the more people insinuated that I couldn't do this, the more fuel it gave me to prove them wrong. Why couldn't I do it? I thought to myself: *I'm not making six figures as a marketing director at a non-profit anyway, so I can recoup that salary in a short enough time. Yes, I am shy, but it might be good for me to get out of my comfort zone. And, you're right, I didn't go to business school, but I'm smart, and I like to learn. I can figure this out.*

I wish I could tell you that I had a succinct checklist for how to begin and each to-do item helped build my business, making it stronger every day. But that's not what happened. I flailed about miserably most days and, as you can guess, it didn't look very pretty. Somehow, however, I found myself cementing important pillars that would support my business for the long haul. From establishing a productive work environment and organizing my day-to-day tasks to learning to set boundaries and navigating business relationships, one morning I did, in fact, wake up and think, "Wow. I have a successful business."

Have I cleared every hurdle in business? No. Have I grown thicker skin for when those hurdles arise? Definitely. Not too long ago, while I was writing this book, I had to fire a client. It was probably only the third client I've had to fire, but I knew how to handle it. It was the first time I didn't need to call my dad to ask him how I should phrase the email. I didn't triple check with my sales coach that this was the right call. I didn't even flinch when the client's response came back – as I'd expected – cold and frustrated. I laughed slightly and shook my head. People are strange, as my mom would say. Life moves on.

Now that you've read this book and know what you'll experience and learn during your first year as an entrepreneur and beyond, you're ready to start your journey. You know how to prepare yourself for this new time in your life, and how to face every challenge along the way.

From this book, you've learned to:

1. Determine what type of workspace will make you productive, establish business hours, and set a personal budget.

2. Develop your client avatar and determine your services for them. We also discussed how to set up your bookkeeping and when to ask for help with important administrative tasks.

3. Implement best practices on scheduling your time as well as build a support network that will encourage you to maintain mental, physical, and emotional health during the transition of owning a business.

4. Market your business to your clients, including how to use social media to your benefit, writing effective content, and building meaningful connections that lead to business.

5. Network effectively both in person and online. We also discussed how to develop your elevator pitch and tactics to beat imposter syndrome.

6. Build business relationships, addressing the types of people you can expect to meet, who will be a supportive business partner, and who may not be.

7. Set boundaries when it comes to establishing your worth (cost) with a client, recognize when it's necessary to fire a toxic client, and how to identify red flags.

8. Overcome setbacks, including how to adapt and overcome. We discussed the ups and downs of entrepreneurship, learning from failure and what to do when you need to change direction.

I would argue that most of these lessons are important for *all* people, regardless of whether you own a business. However, as an entrepreneur, you can expect that living and learning from these lessons, you will successfully navigate the bumpy transition into business ownership. At the end of your first year in business, you can confidently say, "I am my own boss," and mean it. You have set your own schedule, you work with the people that *you* want to work with, you have made new friends, many of whom you do business with on a regular basis, and you have established your reputation as a leader in your industry. People know you. More than that, people trust and respect you; they want to do business with you.

TAKE OUT YOUR PENS

So, you're finally ready to start your entrepreneurial journey and you probably have a good idea what type of business you want to start.

In the white spaces of this book, brainstorm some business names and begin to list the services or products you want to provide. Maybe you list the services/products first, or maybe you start with business names. One will likely feed into the other. Do some research. Are any of these business names taken? Who are your competitors in this space? How can you stand apart? Edit phrases, cut out words, get out the thesaurus, and find like-minded language to get your message across. Once you find a name that speaks to you, your service and/or product offering, and doesn't appear to already be a business name in your industry, circle it. Add several exclamation points and a few hearts around it if you'd like. This is the very first step to becoming a business owner, and it's a big one. Your business is no longer an idea. It's a real thing with a tangible name.

So, what comes next?

Well, I've told you my story. It's time, my friend, to write yours.

Acknowledgements

First and foremost, thank you to Scott MacMillan and the entire Grammar Factory team, especially to my editor Elisa Fernández-Arias, for making this dream a reality.

Second, thank you to my team at Next Page Brand Strategies: Chandler Shea Vogler and Samantha Rosenfeld. I am honored and humbled that you have joined me on this journey.

There are many people I need to thank for giving me the inspiration to write this book. Many of whom came in and out of my life at pivotal times and who taught me important lessons about kindness, faith, and strength. Even those of you who are no longer a part of this journey with me, I will be forever grateful to you:

Anna Smith, Anthony Dalesandro, Ben Baker, Brianna D'Alessio South and Dan South, Blake Bourne and the Veterans Bridge Home Team, Bob Flynn, Bryan Meredith, Cata Frerking, Chaz Seale, Danielle Kleinrichert, Dr. David Bazzetta, Debbie and Dennis D'Alessio, Diane and Jim Gardner, Ebony Stubbs, Ellen Linares, Emily and Scott Cartaya, Emory Simmons, Holly Milanese, Jennifer Moxley, Jim Cusson, Julianna Canfield, Kent Panther, Kristen and Mark DiPietro,

ACKNOWLEDGEMENTS

Madalyn and Garin Grose, Madisyn Zundel, Maria and Norm Miller, Mary Ann and Jim D'Alessio, Matt Burkinshaw, Michelle McDevitt-Askew, Paul Shipley, Nancy Danuser, Nancy Galimi, Nichelle Mosley, Dr. Nicole French, Rochelle Togo-Figa, Shannon Cotton Williams and everyone at Faith Communicators in Charlotte, Shannon Routh, Sharon Blalock, Stacy Cassio, Stephanie Dominguez, Stephanie Landers, Steve Cole, Tamera Green, Tracey Coon, Trish Fries, Wes Howard, and William McKee.

A special thank you to our corporate sponsor Rivus Construction, including Andres Gomez and his team.

And thank you to my first editors and friends, Ken Garfield, Kelly Crum, and Venita James.

To my family:

Seester – Thank you for being my better half. Always.

Momma – Thank you for supporting me and *always* being my Number One cheerleader no matter what.

Daddy – Thank you for being my part-time legal advisor, sales coach, and occasional crisis management team. Your mentorship has meant the world to me.

About the Author

Cassandra D'Alessio is the founder of Next Page Brand Strategies, Inc., a marketing agency dedicated to helping businesses tell authentic stories that build brand loyalty and drive customers to action. Since beginning her writing career at the age of six, Cassandra has leveraged her ability to transform pretty words into powerful messaging that acts as the catalyst for business success at each stage of growth.

Earning her B.A. in Creative Writing at Miami University of Ohio, she proceeded in her academic journey, securing an M.A. in English Literature from the University of Louisville. Thanks to her dedicated focus on trauma writing, her thesis, "To Teach, To Write, To Heal: Trauma Narratives in the Classroom," was honored and presented at the Northeast Modern Language Association Conference in 2012.

After graduating with her Masters, Cassandra continued working in academia as a professor, teaching the craft of writing to students at multiple universities including the University of North Carolina-Charlotte.

Since 2007, she has held a variety of marketing leadership roles. Prior to starting her business, she was the Director of Marketing at a Charlotte non-profit.

Cassandra lives in Charlotte, North Carolina, where she shares her home with her beloved dog, Max. *This Won't Be Pretty* is her first book.

Resources

Below are some helpful resources and additional readings as you begin your entrepreneurial journey. Each of these have helped me during the beginning stages of starting my business, and I hope they prove worthwhile for you, too.

Brown Brené. *Braving the Wilderness: The Quest for True Belonging and the Courage to Stand Alone.* Random House, 2019.

> Brené Brown is known for her research around shame and vulnerability. This book focuses on your identity in the workplace and the importance of remaining authentic to who you are regardless of the work environment in which you find yourself.

Gerber, Michael E. *The E-Myth: Why Most Small Businesses Don't Work and What to Do About It.* Harper Business, 2001.

> A business coach recommended this book to me early on in my entrepreneurial journey. It's a straight-forward, easy read on how most entrepreneurs build their business and the mistakes they make along the way.

"How Great Leaders Inspire Action." Performance by Simon Sinek, *Ted Talk*, Sept. 2009, www.ted.com/talks/ simon_sinek_how_great_leaders_inspire_action?language=en.

> If you haven't seen this Ted Talk, it's a fascinating watch. Sinek discusses how great brands are built and shows the very subtle shift in your own thinking about leadership that will inspire followers and, by extension, gain you clients.

Lamott, Anne. *Bird by Bird.* Anchor Books, 1994.

> This was a favorite "writing" book that I used with my students when I was a professor. Lamott provides real-world advice on how to tackle content writing, especially if it's a task you usually dread. Her popular phrase "shitty first draft" is good advice for both writing and life.

Rackham, Neil. *Spin Selling.* McGraw-Hill, 1988.

> Although the advertising examples are from the 1980s, this is by far the best sales book I have read. Rackham discusses the types of questions you should be asking during the sales process that can be adapted to any industry.

Sandberg, Sheryl. *Lean In: Women, Work, and the Will to Lead.* Random House UK, 2015.

> Sheryl Sandberg's book discusses how women can build a satisfying career along with her own personal anecdotes and research that

seeks to change the conversation around what women can't do to what they can.

Shaw, Jeffrey. *LINGO: Discover Your Ideal Customer's Secret Language and Make Your Business Irresistible.* Creative Warriors Press, 2018.

This book, as its title suggests, focuses on the language you use to describe your product or service. From whether or not you include a dollar sign in your pricing to how to create your own daily affirmations, this book discusses language in all forms in your business.